Jesus and Those Bodacious Women

Jesus and Those Bodacious Women

Life Lessons from One Sister to Another

Linda H. Hollies

———— ∾ ————

Pilgrim Press
Cleveland, Ohio

Pilgrim Press, Cleveland, Ohio 44115
© 1998 by Linda H. Hollies

05 04 03 02   5

Library of Congress Cataloging-in-Publication Data

Hollies, Linda H.
    Jesus and those bodacious women : life lessons from one
sister to another / Linda H. Hollies.
        p.   cm.
    Includes bibliographical references.
    ISBN 0-8298-1246-6 (pbk. : alk. paper)
    1. Afro-American women—Religious life.   2. Christian life—
Methodist authors. I. Title.
BR563.N4H65 1998
248.8'43—dc21

This book is dedicated to the sisters of Woman to Woman Ministries, Inc. These women are a group of God-sent, bodacious sisters who have loved me through periods of time when I needed to revisit frequently the lessons of becoming a bodacious woman again!

May God forever bless and keep my daughters in ministry, Jacqui Ford, Sandi Adams, Darlene Webster, Cheryl Williams, Belyinda Johnson, and Tracy Flagg; my encouraging prayer-warrior mothers, Lucille Brown, Ray Margaret Jackson, Ruby Earven; and sisters, Daisybelle Thomas-Quinney, Vera Jo Edington, Janet Hopkins, Linda Boston, Lillian Gibbs, Joyce Wallace, Telma Pryor, Harlene Harden, Beverly Garvin, Madine Blakley, Michelle Cobb, and Ida Easley; and my superbodacious pastor, Eleanor L. Miller. Without them my journey could have been stuck in mediocrity!

CONTENTS

PREFACE

The word "bodacious" means unmistakable, remarkable, and noteworthy. When Jesus Christ comes into the life of a woman, she becomes bodacious. I learned this from my own life experience.

If you have read the story of my life, recorded in my book *Inner Healing for Broken Vessels*, you already know that I was the victim of my own father's incest and that my mother "overlooked" his sin. Childhood traumas of this nature do not tend to make individuals bold, outstanding, and outgoing. They tend to produce shy, retiring, and withdrawn people who want to hide their shameful past. They wear masks and use a disguise to pretend that all is well while dying slowly on the inside. This was the life I lived until the age of twenty-seven. Then, I met Jesus Christ. I had a personal, born-again experience that changed my life forever. I discovered love. I found freedom. I was given power. I became a bodacious woman. My life has not been the same since.

As I have read and studied Scripture, I have found that God has always had bodacious women tucked away for us to find. The male compilers of the canon could not erase their remarkable feats. When I went away to seminary, I was taught the principles for "digging" beneath the words on the page to track down what was going on and who was being talked to and about when a given passage was written. I learned much about the work of bodacious women.

These events—the touch of Christ in my life and my educational pursuits—have combined to make me a student-learner-teacher-preacher, for the liberation of the Christ must be shared with women who have been hurt and feel small, insignificant, and alone. So, inspired by the Holy Spirit, I have compiled some lessons for you about bodacious women in Scripture. May another view of their lives bless you. May a different slant on their witness inform you. May new lessons from their journey make yours more smooth. Read these stories for information. Digest them for inspiration. Use them for motivation. Then, tell them to your sisters, for I am persuaded that Jesus

Christ wants each one of us who is called a Christian woman to be a bodacious woman.

Author's Note about Scriptures

I take great personal liberty with Scripture! I believe it was written for me. And I know it needs to have inclusive language to include all of us. So I have attempted to be true to documenting the sources of every scriptural reference, using the New International Version translation for most of my references. However, this version is not wholly inclusive in its language. Therefore, I pray you will be indulgent as you read your select version and find it does not say "exactly" what I have stated. It's what I saw and felt was intended!

Acknowledgments

A book is never written in isolation. All the persons who touch, influence, inspire, and even hinder your life help you in the writing process. The lessons you have learned and the individuals who taught you hover over your shoulders, waiting to see if you mastered the materials. In the same way that "it takes a village to raise a child," it takes your entire community to write a book. And, it takes bodacious women in the community to role-model correct behavior for little girls.

I am thankful to my "life community" for my personal experiences and awareness of the journey of forgiveness. Many are the charitable and gracious souls who have forgiven me when I have stumbled, blundered, and just plain messed up. I have been picked up, lifted up, forgiven, and blessed to grow and to become. It is in community that I have become a bodacious woman.

My family of origin heads this list of folks who helped write this book. My grandmothers, Lucinda Weston, Eunice Wade, Ethel Kellom, and Lessie Bell King, live in me, speak to me, and continue to admonish and cheer me as they watch from the realms of glory. My Big Daddy, Dock Wade, is with them, and I appreciate the loving role modeling he provided. My parents, James and Doretha Adams, gave me life and granted me the necessary lessons that have taught me to hold on to God's unchanging hand. My aunt, Barbara Ruth Weston, taught me, by example, the art of meditation, relaxing, releasing, and letting go of yesterday's pain. Church mothers and community mothers have played vital roles in my becoming. Especially dear to my heart are Mother Lula Smith and Mother Louise Holliway. All of these people now await me on the "other side." "Miss" Ethel Sims, a neighbor-mother, Hortense House, teacher-mother, and Dr. Della Burt, professor-mother each taught me how to "strut my stuff." I pray that I teach their lessons well.

My siblings and extended family are the rich soil that has nurtured my soul. For Jacquie, Bob, and Troy; Riene, Tony, Lynne, Michael, and

Missy; Regina, Arthur, Raymond, Ibn, and Millicent; James Jr., Jeanette, Noah, and Mohanna; Eddie, Onnette, Eddie Jr., and Candace; David, Kim, Dave Jr., and Ean; and Robert Tyrone, I give God thanks and praise. The loving support of my "awesome uncle" Clenton Weston has upheld, supported, and encouraged me through the years.

Finally, my husband, Chuck; my daughter, Grian; her sons, Giraurd and Gamel; and my sons, Greg and Grelon, have each taught me lessons and learned, because of me, how to live bodaciously. My family is another name for love. They inspire and sustain this bodacious woman in ministry. God gave them as gifts in my life.

Bodacious Black Women
Twinkling Stars

(Dedicated to Joan Rebecca Coursey)

In the Origin of articulated history, the Divine
     Designer
gathered rich, dark, bittersweet chocolate, and
     mixed it with love,
intelligence, and dynamism, to fashion the Black
     Woman.
The entire human race issued forth from her
     abundant womb.
The Creator watched her production and declared,
     "Very good!"

A palatial garden in Africa was the world's first
     home. And, with amazing
accuracy, our mother named the world. Gifted with a
     sharp mind,
keen intellect, and unbelievably perceptive wit, Eve
     was curious, intuitive, and inquisitive.
For a Woman of Color was the earliest navigator
     and explorer, since brilliance

always seeks to enlarge her capacity and to expand
her potential.

Eve was a seeker of truth, a delighter in beauty, and
wise beyond belief.
She negotiated with evil principalities, pushed past
her boundaries,
and sought to include all of humankind as she
worked on issues of justice.

Other Black Women, like her, have been assigned
to the culture of the unheard,
condemned to the society of the unseen, and
banished to the continent of invisibility.
Yet, they have continued their explorations,
unnoticed and unheralded by the world.
Silently, they have hummed simple songs, engaging the Mystery of Life.

Quietly, they have twinkled in their places and the
Divine has never
left them alone. The Ancient of Days has preserved
their souls.
And the Holy Spirit's power has caused their
brilliance to touch every life.

Definitions cannot contain them. Imposed
limitations cannot imprison them.

Black Women were created to reign!
The royal blood of creation pulsates in their veins.
 The thirst for knowledge
rules in their hearts. They will not sacrifice their
 heritage.
 Their stories will live on!

Proud progeny of Africa, we are daughters,
 mothers, sisters, wives,
divorced, single, gay, and straight. We are
 preachers,
teachers, engineers, actors, construction workers
 too. We are
students, learners, and plain, good, Black Women!
 We are Sistahs,
honey childs, and Sweet Honey in the Rock! We
 are kin to Zipporah,
Hagar, and the Candace of Ethiopia. Created to
 rule, we have been forced to serve.
We have served Creation well!
With queenly bearing and the dignity of sacred
 saints, we have offered
 our best. Our breasts have nourished the world.
 The hands of
Black Women have rocked the cradles of the most
 powerful and the least significant.
The songs of Black Women have changed the
 most recalcitrant hearts.

Only the ledgers of time without end will detail
the exploits
of Black Women. For these daughters of dark
earth continue to
call us to shine. Our eyes are on the prize. Never
will our heads be bowed.
Our salvation is assured. Our names are written
on high!
So, "Twinkle, twinkle, little stars," our God knows
who we really are!
We are some beautiful, bad, and *bodacious*
women!

Linda H. Hollies
August 1997
United Methodist Clergywomen's Consultation

INTRODUCTION
MEET MS. CHIPPIE

Chippie never knew what hit her. One moment she was perched high, queen of her world, secure and singing her heart out. But her owner decided that today was cage-cleaning day and she would do it the quick way, with a vacuum cleaner. As the last attachment was snapped on and the cage door opened, the phone rang. Turning to answer, the owner heard a "swoosh." Poor Chippie had been sucked into the vacuum. Hanging up the phone, the woman quickly tore open the bag, and there sat poor Chippie, dirty and stunned but still alive.

Grabbing the little bird, the owner rushed into the bathroom and turned on the faucet to rinse Chippie off. But she felt shivers shaking that tiny body. So, doing what any compassionate owner would do, she grabbed the hair dryer and hit Chippie full blast with hot air. Chippie never knew what hit her! In less than two minutes, her world had been turned upside down. She had been sucked in, washed up, and blown over. A couple of days later, the friend who had initiated the call checked on Chippie. "Well," her owner replied, "Chippie doesn't sing much anymore."[1]

Can any of you identify with Chippie? I know I can, for life is not fair. Life does not have a set of failure-proof rules. The bottom can drop out of your world without a moment's notice. It takes only one phone call from the police station, asking about your child. It takes only one county office delivering the divorce petition to you. It takes only news of the government's plans to downsize and close your facilities. It takes only one meeting in your boss's office, or one knock on your door with bad news.

It is almost impossible to believe that one mammogram reading, one prostate test, or one culture report can throw your whole world into chaos and leave you feeling stunned, sucked in, washed over, and blown away. A Chippie moment will steal your song. A Chippie moment will shake your faith. A Chippie moment will truly rock your world. And if you think about your own life and those of your girlfriends, you know that Chippie is alive and well today.

We can gather for a time of professional development. We can search to glean new information, to fine-tune our skills. But life is not kind. Bad news, hard blows, family problems, and personal issues travel with each one of us on a daily basis. Some painful brokenness is alive and well at every seminar, workshop, or church service you attend. Anywhere people gather, they are in a room full of wounded folks. Friends, I have discovered a well-kept secret. We can train, get education, receive promotions, and take the executive escalator to success, but we cannot hide from nor escape life's Chippie experiences.

Crisis has no geographic boundaries. Crisis has no ethnic or cultural restrictions. Crisis has no regard for money, position, status, or title. Crisis will find you, regardless of where you travel. Crisis will cause everybody to be equal in feeling helpless, anxious, and confused. And crisis will make the best of us look like lost sheep without a shepherd. But there's good news for bodacious women. Jesus has already come to show us how to look with discerning eyes and see the pain around us and within our own souls. Jesus Christ came to show us how to pray and how to care. Jesus Christ came to give us the power, the authority, and the mandate to intervene with loving, healing care for both the Chippie among us and the Chippie within us. For Jesus Christ came so that we might become bodacious women!

I clearly remember my first full day on the job as the first African American pastor of a two-thousand-member, wealthy, Anglo, suburban, United Methodist church. With the exception of my husband and grandson, my surroundings were totally Anglo. It was truly a strange land. All of us in the North Illinois Conference were anxious over the bishop's decision to make this cross-cultural appointment. All of us were experiencing our individual and collective Chippie moments. It was bad for me, until I closed my office door on the first day. I sat at my desk, stunned and overwhelmed. With my big, bad, efficient, and scared self, I cried like a baby. A gentle, hesitant knock struck my door. As I wiped my eyes, repaired my makeup, and tried to look occupied, I called, "Come in."

"Pastor Linda, what time will you be at the parsonage this evening? I have to deliver your dinner, and I want it to be hot."

I went from stunned to delighted in a single moment. I moved from despair to hope with that one tentative intervention. I was delivered from sadness to singing because someone showed healing, loving care. For genuine love has no color, gender, or age limitations.

With this intervention of one hesitant knock on my door, this Chippie had her song back! Jo Mazik brought me an egg quiche, and this black woman loves meat. Jo Mazik brought prune muffins, and this black woman loves nuts and berries. Jo Mazik intervened with healing, loving care, which this black woman pastor sorely needed and accepted fully and eagerly.

Beloved, Chippie moments keep on coming, for life is not fair. But healing offered in loving care, even hesitantly, can restore a song and help a wounded bird fly again. I hope you will not be too surprised to discover that the Holy Spirit has taught me much from this experience. And I pray that you will be open and alert to the ministering opportunities that show up in each of our lives. We must learn how to minister to each other. We must begin to experience what it means to be soul friends. We are privileged to practice inner healing as broken vessels. We can be deliberate about our care for each other. And Jesus wants us bodacious women to encounter the stranger within ourselves and come to know her in a more intimate manner.

Wherever you go today, look around. Be attuned to the spirit of discernment that allows you to look beyond a smiling face and view the broken heart and wounded spirit that lies just beneath that mask. In every place, even in your life space, there are Chippies who have been sucked in, washed up, and blown over. Thank God for an opportunity to be involved in a healing ministry to another. Thank God for Jesus, who has chosen us to intervene in the lives of stunned and wounded birds. Thank God for Jesus, whose resurrection power is available so that by our love and care and intervention in the lives of each other, we might help Chippie mount her perch and sing again. The time to begin our soul-to-soul ministry is *now*!

Just Between Us

- What was the last episode that "stole your song"?
- What did it feel like?
- Had you ever experienced those feelings before?
- What or who helped to cheer you, to right your world, to allow you to "hum"?

- Can you hear the song of other sisters
  when you cannot sing?
- Are you in a support group of sisters?
  a Bible study group of sisters?
  a church school class of sisters?
- Do you think this could help you
  reclaim your song?

Suggestions

Do you know of any sister who is going through an extremely distressing time in her life today? Go to your local card shop and buy a card just for her! Do you know of a single mom with no family close around? Call and ask if you could come and spend a day to give her a break. Make her day! Singing is often done in rounds. Do something to help another get her song back, and watch something happen to bring a song back to your heart!

chapter one

≈

TILL YOU DO ME RIGHT
THE MAKING OF A BODACIOUS WOMAN

Jeremiah 18:1–11

I really like the words to the song "Till You Do Me Right."[1] It is a song about a relationship that has gone bad. It is a song about someone's feelings being disregarded and his or her personhood being disrespected. It is a song about somebody who has a good measure of self-esteem and requires other folks to treat him or her right. It is a song about someone who seems to know what it feels like to have been messed with, mistreated, lied to, and hurt because of the lies and duplicity of a partner who has caused deep pain.

The songwriter seems to have had some first-hand experience with a person who had taken him or her for granted and neglected to consider that a person's ways are eventually found out. The song is definitely about a love that has gone sour.

The song is from the heart of a person who has been betrayed, who has known what it's like to forgive one incident and even another, only to find out that the relationship has been a lie all the time. This person sounds like an individual who has cried long into the night and woke up to meet those same tears. This person writes as one who has tried to fool himself or herself time after time and keeps getting slapped in the face with the reality of being dishonest with oneself. I know from personal experience about the words of this song. I have been there and have surely done that!

As long as you are asleep and in a fog about an individual, your heart sings and your emotions ride high. You can stay on a cloud and imagine what life is going to be like with this awesome individual. You spend time talking and sharing and dreaming and planning. You dare to risk being intimate, not only allowing that person to enter your sacred sexual space but also letting him or her have access to your inner thoughts, your innermost secrets, and your untold hopes. Oh, it's heaven to be able to talk seriously and to be open and honest and to believe that you have been listened to with attention. It's wonderful to be in love!

We all have a fantasy of finding that special someone who will love us without conditions, who will care for us no matter what, and who will be there for us when the chips are down. We want passion. We want excitement. We want sexual thrills. But more than anything, we want someone to love us gently and to be committed to us for the long haul. It's part of the human dream, part of the human psyche. Love is what makes the world go round. No matter where you travel, no matter what the race, tribe, or ethnic group, there is a sexual attraction and a mating ritual and a game that we play.

Love sells. It sells books. It sells movies and videos. It sells clothing and perfumes. It sells cars and even vacuum cleaners. Its rates high as an advertiser. It rates high as a featured attraction in lectures, workshops, and seminars. Everybody wants love! Love can be wonderful. Love can be special. Love can be grand. Love can open your nose and cause you to do crazy things. Love can make you behave like an imbecile. Love can make you go out on a limb and get yourself in debt trying to please and win over the object of your love. Love can make you compromise your values and do things you swore you never would. Love can make you toss away your ethics and get

you involved in things you would not commonly
do. Love can make you crazy. Love can make you
stupid. Love can make a fool out of the best of
us. For we all need someone to love. And, more
important, we need someone to love us.

Love can go wrong. Sometimes we do not
make the best choices about lovers. Sometimes
we allow our emotions to run wild without engaging our heads. Sometimes our heart says one
thing, our rational thought says something else,
and confusion sets in. Sometimes we begin to
suspect that things are not what we thought they
were. Sometimes we begin to get the feeling that
we are being played. Sometimes the little things
just do not add up. The stories do not jibe. The
words do not ring true. There is no consistency
between the words being said and the feelings we
are experiencing. A little nagging voice begins to
say, "Watch out." A little whisper in our ear says,
"Be careful." A little nudge in our spirit says,
"This ain't right." And once awakened, a sleeping fool cannot be put back to sleep.

I was talking with another clergy member
about one of her female parishioners, whose husband of thirty-two years had played her once too
often. He had three other women, and babies by
each one. The women had credit cards with his

name, and the bills came to his home. The wife had gotten tired, and the husband had to go. He left a number where he could be reached, and she did not call for many days. But love will make you change your mind. So, she dialed the number, and a woman answered the phone. When the husband came to the phone, the wife asked, "Who was that?" Can you believe that he tried to make her think that she was crazy by telling her that no woman had answered the phone? What was more shocking was the fact that he had played that game before and she had fallen for it! Love can make you doubt your sanity.

But one day the light will click on. One day the sun will break through the fog in your mind. One day you simply wake up. Things begin to add up for you, you begin to see clearly, and you simply know what you know and know that you know it. First, you begin to give out little hints. Then you begin to give just the eye clue that says, "I'm not as dumb as I look." Finally, you get tired of the game playing and begin to sing the song:

Ain't nothing good gonna happen to you, till you do me right.
I don't want to talk to you, till you do me right.
I don't want to hear you call my name, till you do me right.

Cause ain't nothing good gonna happen to you, till
   you do me right.[2]

Girlfriend, you have become a bodacious woman!

Nobody wants to be made a fool. Nobody
wants to be played. Nobody wants to believe that
they were dumb enough to fall for the old con
game of being taken for a sucker. We do strange
things when people take advantage of our affec-
tions. We act in peculiar ways when we know
that someone is trying to use us for his or her
advantage. We are likely to hurt, get back at, or
even kill a person who misuses our affection.
Alienation of affection is a serious offense in a
court of law, and divorces have been granted on
this charge. Murder cases have been won when
the jury buys the defense of a love gone wrong
that affects the defendant's judgment, causing that
person to kill out of temporary insanity because
of the anguish.

We can all understand a scorned lover being
hurt. We can all comprehend a scorned lover taking revenge. But we cannot fathom our God being a lover who will turn on us. God longs for us
to be true lovers in our personal relationship. God
desires that we would be genuine, straight-up,
authentic, and real when we say that we love God.

God wants words that are backed up with action. God wants sincerity of motive, honest expression, and deeds that will let the world know that we really are serious about this love.

God is the ultimate lover, who chose us when we had nothing to offer. This love came our way when we were downright ugly, dirty, filthy, and lost in our sin. When we were in the gutter of life, God came and picked us up, turned us around, and claimed us with love. God has been a generous lover. God has been a tender lover. God has been a kind lover. God has always been there for us. God has continued to make ways for us. God has been faithful to us. And God has loved us so much that God's only begotten child was sent to die in our place. You cannot doubt God's love; it has been proven. You cannot fault God's love; it has been steadfast. You cannot deny God's love; it has been rock steady. But God's people have always had a habit of playing God for a fool. God's people have a reputation of walking off, being unfaithful, and even having affairs with other gods. God's people have a tendency to lie, cheat, and try to swindle the greatest lover who has ever been. We think we can play with God's love and get away with it.

The prophet Jeremiah was deeply involved in the political life of the people of God. He prophesied under the reigns of many kings, both in the united kingdom of Israel and after the kingdom was split in two. Jeremiah announced judgment on God's backsliding folks. Jeremiah pronounced doom if they didn't fall on their faces and repent of their evil ways. Jeremiah had a message from God to those who continued to play God for a fool. Prophets always received their message straight from God and always began their message by saying, "This is the Word of the Lord."

Jeremiah wanted the nation to understand that the message was hard to hear, although it was not difficult to understand. The message was filled with warnings and impending judgment, but it was from God. Jeremiah did not want to bring it; he did not want to say it, and he did not want to be around to see it come true. However, he was only the messenger, and the message had to be delivered. Jeremiah came to tell the church of the living God that God said, "Nothing good is gonna happen to you till you do me right. I don't want to talk with you, so don't bother to pray till you decide to do me right. I don't want to hear you call my name, with your two-faced ways, until you do me right. Cause nothing good is gonna happen to you until you do me right!"

Jeremiah told the people how he had been sent by God to go and watch a potter spin a vessel on the wheel. As Jeremiah watched a master craftsman at work, the pot fell. If you have ever worked with clay, you know it's pliable and weak, not strong and hardy. So, even in the making, the pot was spoiled in the potter's hand. But rather than throwing the pot away, rather than saying it was worthless, rather than saying it was no-account and useless, the potter took that spoiled vessel and began to reshape and remake it into a more beautiful vessel than it had been previously.

It is our human tendency to want to destroy something that is deformed. When our relationships go sour, we want to pull each other down, take away every material thing, and wreck each other's lives. We do not want the other person, but we do not want anybody else to want that person either. We like to reject those who have hurt us. We want to turn our backs on them and to write them off as worthless. Thank God for the Potter who does not have our human frailties. Thank God for a second chance. Thank God for the opportunity to be reworked instead of destroyed.

We know that we are not living up to our fullest potential. We are scorning the Lover of our souls. We are rejecting true love. But, the Potter wants to make us over again. The Potter wants to do a new job on us, not to destroy us but to make our love relationship stronger, better, and more committed. We know that we are playing God. We know that we are not being fair. We know that we attend church without really worshiping God. We realize that we take the holy sacrament without really meaning to be disciples. We understand that we take God's breath, time, energy, and strength, and we go to work to receive the monetary blessings that God has stored up for us, and then we take God's time and money and give it to our other lovers!

"Reverend, I do not have time to work with the children's ministry; I'm so tired after working all day." "Reverend, I just cannot get here for Bible study; it's my bowling/bridge/sorority meeting/football night." "Reverend, I cannot tithe, but I consistently increase my pledge." "Reverend, I cannot tithe; I owe too many people, I have too many bills, I have kids in school." Well, God got tired of the excuses. God got tired of the old rap. God had enough of being lied to over and over again. God said, "Look, I am a potter shaping evil against you and devising a plan against you."

"Wait, God—you are love. Wait, God—you are gentle. Wait, God—you are meek and mild-mannered. Wait, God—you are simply too nice to sound like that." But God is a lover who has been spurned. God is a lover who has been rejected. God is a lover who has been played over and over again. This is a warning for the game players. This is a warning for those who continue to want to play church. This is a warning for those who will not be serious about their relationship with God. God is not ignorant of what we do; God is not crazy. God sees. God is watching. And God is warning us that our evil ways will be judged.

The Potter wants to work out that ultimate purpose for your life. If it takes hard times and difficulties, God will send them your way. God wants us to be vessels of beauty, pure both inside and out. If it takes long nights and difficult days to get you to return to your lover, God is willing to allow that to happen.

The troubles, the difficulties, the misery, and the trials are meant not to punish you but to draw you back to the arms of the Beloved. God loves you so much. God wants so much to have you in an open and honest relationship. God wants to be intimate with you and to work on you, from the inside out. God wants to shine in your life. God wants the victory to be yours. God wants you to be the most dazzling, brilliant, and awesome display of divine love. God wants you to be a bodacious woman.

You know how people want to show off their best china. We want to display our best porcelain and crystal. We want the world to see the most beautiful and most cherished articles that we possess. Just so, God wants the world to see Christ in our lives. And this happens only when we are in love with and devoted fully to our God.

Love is always about correction. Love is always about relationship. Love is always about having your best in mind. So, Love told Jeremiah, "I am the Potter and I want the people to know I want no more game playing. For nothing good is gonna happen to them till they do me right. I don't want to hear from them until they decide to do me right. I don't want to hear them call my name till they do me right. For nothing good is gonna happen to them till they do me right!"

Then, Love told Jeremiah how the people could do right. "All you have to do," said

Jeremiah, "is straighten up and fly right. If you will turn now, all of you, from your evil ways and amend your ways and your doings, Love will do you right! Repent, change, do differently from what you are doing. There is a better way. There is a new way that leads to more abundant life. The choice is up to you." With just one turn toward God in honesty and earnestness, the bodacious woman within you is released and your world is a much better place. So, always keep in mind the voice of God saying, "Nothing good is gonna happen to you till you do me right!"

Just Between Us

- Has somebody done you wrong lately?
- Who?
- How did that make you feel?
- Do you need to work on some honest forgiveness in your life?
- Have you been playing around on God— you know, not really living like you know you should?
- Have you been "playing church," attending but not being active in ministry?
- Do you need to work on some honest repentance in your life?

- Have you seriously "fallen in love" with Jesus lately, spending time together, whispering sweet nothings, singing love songs?
- When you decide to "do right by him," do you think things might go better for you?
- Could the situation you are in be God's way of developing more of your potential?
- Can you imagine what your life might be like if you treated God "more right"?

Suggestions

Just for the rest of today, try making Jesus the center of your world. Speak to Jesus more tenderly and more often. Consult Jesus before making another decision. Over and over whisper how much you really love Jesus.

Get an old shoe box out of the closet and gift wrap it with beautiful paper. Fill it with drugstore sample-sized boxes of creams, soft soaps, toothpaste, and "stuff" from your hotel stays (I collect them just for this purpose). Add some fingernail polish, colognes, and hair dressings. Now take the box over to the local women's shelter, and ask to visit with the last woman admitted for safety. We treat God right when we decide to take the time and opportunity to do for the "least."

chapter two

≈

A LIVING PRAYER
EVE

Genesis 1

In the beginning, God stepped out into space and looked around at the nothingness, at the chaos and emptiness all around, and God said, "I will make me a world." As far as the eye of God could see, there was blackness everywhere; the blackness was deeper than a thousand midnights in a cypress swamp. God said, "I will have light." So, the thunder rolled, the lightning flashed, and the sun appeared in the sky. God's "I will" brought the moon and the stars and the galaxies whirling and swirling in the skies. God's "I will" was a clap of hands that created the Himalayan Mountains. God's "I will" was the batting of eyes that gave us oceans and seas, rivers and lakes. God's "I will" brought the rose springing through the crevice of rocky ground and little daisies pointing their heads toward the heavenly skies. God's "I will" decreed trees and forest, meadows and rippling grass. At the sound of God's "I will," the cooling rains came down. The wonder of creation, the majesty of our world, and the splendor of the universe were designed by God's divine will.

Then the "I will" of the Heavenly Council came together and decided to create human beings in their image. So, like a great mother bending over her child, the God of eternity stooped down and gathered a lump of clay. Molding and shaping the clay into form, with a gentleness and a sureness that were clear, the Creator designed our first parents. Then, looking at these fine specimens of humanity, God thought and thought about the gifts that the humans would need for life. Then the Ancient of Days breathed "I will" into the nostrils of the lifeless, and we became living souls. Amen. Amen.[1]

You are not a loser in the game of life. You are not doomed to come in last in the race with time. You are not forever destined to be one of the have-nots. It makes no difference what is going on in your life right this moment. It really does not matter what you do or do not have in the bank on deposit today. God does not care that you are overweight, too thin, too dark, or have no rhythm. What matters to God is what you are doing with that divine "I will" that was planted inside you "in the beginning." This "I will" can take you from where you are to where you ought to be in life. This "I will" can move you from the dumps to the heights. This "I will" can change your life and jump-start your future. You just have to access the "I will" inside yourself. The difference between the haves and the have-nots is the amount of "I will" they choose to activate in their lives. The difference between those who make strides and achievements in their lives and those who don't is in direct proportion to the "I will" that they allow to motivate and inspire them on a day-to-day basis. The difference between the movers and shakers and those who simply plod along, limping through life, is that the movers and shakers are propelled by their "I will."

I will make a difference! I will be a bodacious woman! I will have dominion over my world. I will have an inspiring career. I will help someone along the way. I will love myself and attract love into my world. I will serve God with every breath I take. I will depend upon the power of the Holy Spirit to lead me and guide me along the way. I will live a life of victory. I will live a life in which the good of the universe is drawn unto me. I will have a body that is healthy and in divine order. I will have a companion who will compliment me, cherish me, and care for me in the way that I need. I will have friends who are climbers and achievers. I will dream impossible dreams and fight unbeatable foes. I will! I will! For my will is a gift from God. My will is a mandate for me to choose the creative, the artistic, and the beautiful for my life. My will is my ability to change my circumstances, to follow my divine path, and to live a life that is pleasing to God. It's possible because I choose to use my "I will."

Jesus was chosen and anointed by God. Jesus was filled with the Holy Spirit and with power. Jesus went about doing good, making a difference, and bringing joy, life, and beauty wherever he went. He did it because God was with him. He chose to live out of the "I will": "I will change the circumstances of the little and insignificant ones. I will bring life where evil has brought decay and death. I will take the common and ordinary and show them the significant and the mystical, even in the symbols of water and bread and grape juice. I will show them how to live a life seeking justice. I will show them how to live a life of prayer." Jesus was the servant of God. He was directed and upheld by God. He was God's delight.

Jesus did not delight God because of his material wealth. He was born in a stable and housed in a manger. So where we begin life and what we accumulate in life do not delight God. Jesus did not delight God because of the great society within which he climbed the social ladder. He chose the scum of the society as friends and the uneducated as disciples. So our strides up the corporate ladder and our seeking to be in the blue book of noted society do not delight God. It could not have been the position in life to which Jesus climbed or the education that he achieved that delighted God, for Jesus was a common carpenter who worked with his hands. So our degrees, our fraternities, our sororities, and our lodges do not delight God. Jesus was the delight of God because he lived a life of prayer.

A life of prayer is a life that depends on God. A life of prayer is a life in which we do the right thing even when the opposite is the common way. A life of prayer is one in which we make good and godly decisions even in bad and ungodly situations. A life of prayer is one in which we follow ethical behavior, not because somebody is watching but as a way of pleasing God. Prayer is not simply words, not begging, not just talking and listening to God. Prayer is a way of living. Prayer is a lifestyle. Prayer is living out of ethical behavior. And each of us is called to a life of prayer, for we are followers of Jesus Christ.

It is hard, it is not fair, and it is not easy. But we are God's servants. We are called and chosen of God. We are given a direct breath of "I will" and the power of the Holy Spirit to make things happen. The Holy Spirit is God alive in you. So, you have the power to do right, even when it is popular to do wrong. You have the power to do right, although it's hard. It's not fair, it does not make sense, and it does not make you feel good. You do it because it brings healing to the world you are creating. You do it because it brings healing to those who are watching your life. You do it because healing brings about justice, and justice brings in the realm of God.

You do right because you have been chosen, you have been selected by God, you have been elected as the one. Why you? Because God chose you. Out of all who could have been chosen, God picked you. And not only did God pick you, but God will also uphold you. Why? Because God delights in you—not in what you have or have not done; not in what you have or have not achieved; not in what you do or do not do. God simply delights in your being. Because you are, Gods loves you. Because God gives you breath, God loves you. Because you were not aborted or miscarried or thrown away on some garbage dump and allowed to die, God loves you. Simply because you are a divine creation, with "I will" planted inside you as a gift from "In the Beginning," God delights in you.

It is powerful, it is awesome, it is breathtaking to know that I delight God. It is authoritative, it is overwhelming, it is monumental to know that God delights in me, takes pleasure and joy in me. When I'm down, it pulls me up. When I'm scared, it gives me courage. When I'm disappointed, it lifts my spirits. When I have messed up and failed, it allows me to go on. When I want to quit, it is my kick start. When I want to back up, it is the push from behind that sends me ahead. When I want to do wrong, it is the force that says, "Do the right thing." When I am leaning toward the popular choice, it's the reminder of whose I am. I am God's servant. I am God's child. I am chosen by God. I am a bodacious woman.

When you do not choose me, that's all right.

When you do not affirm me, that's all right. When you do not like me, that's all right. When life acts up, that's all right. When the clouds are heavy and there are tears in my eyes, that's all right. For I remember that I am God's child. God is with me. I am not alone. And I have the "I Will" of creation living within me. It is the lift in my life. It is the joy in my song. It is the new beginning for every day. It is the hope for tomorrow. It is the resurrection in every death.

For others decided that Jesus was not popular enough. They decided that he was not in the "in group" enough. They decided that he had no good and worthy qualities. So they hung him high and they stretched him wide. They nailed him to the cross and they watched him die. But the "I Will" was not finished. The "I Will" belonged to God. The "I Will" rose again. And the "I Will" lives in me. "He walks with me and he talks with me and he tells me that I am his own."[2] So, I will make a difference. I will sing my song. I will tell my story. I will. I will. I will!

Just Between Us

Been feeling like a "loser" lately? Try sitting someplace quiet and engaging your "I will" in conversation. Most of us run around doing meaningless things, trying to fill empty time in order to be fulfilled, without knowing what we were created to do. The "I will" was intentional about your creation and has a definite purpose for your life. When you begin to follow your heart, listen to your dream, and pay attention to your gut instead of doing what is comfortable, life will take off in creative and explosive bursts of wonder and surprise!

Suggestions

See whether anyone is available at your place of employment to help you discover your life's vocation. Or find a spiritual director (through the Catholic diocese in your area, for example), a person who has been trained to listen to you and to help you discern what the Holy Spirit is saying to you.

chapter three

MARY MAGDALENE CAN FLY!

John 20:1–18

Mary Hamilton's book *The People Could Fly* tells the wonderful story about a great people who had magical powers.[1] They could fly! They didn't need flying machines or airborne contraptions. But with their songs, their inner strength, and their mental capabilities, their spirits would soar, and often their bodies would join their spirits in sailing above the terrain. The people thought nothing of this ability. They thought everybody was like them. They lived with difficulties, they fought nature to survive, and they had enemies both within and without; but something so strong inside gave them the power to rise above situations and circumstances. With the powerful gift of memory they remembered that once upon a time they had the ability to fly.

This is the call of Easter. This is the call of God's church. We need to remember that we were divinely designed by God to become bodacious women. Every Ash Wednesday, we are called to remember that we are dust. We were created from dust, and it is to dust that we will return. Remember. The road back to God requires that through a series of scriptures calling us, we re-hear, retell, and reflect upon the story of our faith and remember the love of Jesus for us. As we kneel to wash feet and stand to celebrate the first Passover meal, which has become our communion, we are challenged to remember. Every Easter is another call to remember. We are to remember that the people could fly! For we are an Easter people, and rising is our constant theme of praise.

This story is told in three of the Gospels. The crucifixion is over, the funeral has been held, and a period of lamenting by the women has been completed. "Early on the first day of the week, while it was still dark, Mary Magdalene came to the tomb and saw that the stone had been removed from the tomb" (John 20:1). This woman, our sister, had been at the crucifixion. She had stood and watched the Lover of her soul die a cruel and ignominious death. She had been at the funeral, a very small funeral for Jesus attended by three female followers, one male disciple, and two Gentiles. In a day when the world felt that women should be seen and not heard, should be responsible to the authority of some man and remain socially invisible, Mary had defied convention. She had acted out of character for a woman. She had been in places where the brothers had dared not be seen. Mary had been there because she was a bodacious woman.

Mary Magdalene, the Bible records, had a bad reputation. It is reputed that Jesus had driven seven devils out of her. Some say she had been a woman of ill repute, a woman of the night, a woman of disrespect. We have to remember that anyone who was not predictable was labeled "possessed." Anything people cannot explain, prove, or understand, they want to label. But Jesus had looked beyond Mary's labels. Jesus had risked his reputation to save her from hers. We don't know what kind of demons she supposedly had, but, being a woman, I do know the kinds of demons that plague me: the demons of doubt, despair, discouragement, defeat, depression, debilitating weariness, and disbelief. And there are many more I could name. For the demons are real. The demons are on the job. The demons come to stop us from rising and flying. The demons come to make sure that we don't remember.

But Jesus had loved Mary despite whatever mess she had been in before. Jesus had looked beyond her human faults and had seen her essential need for someone to love her with an extravagant love. So, it is no surprise that Mary was searching for the one who had dared to believe in her goodness, her value, and the imago Dei within her. Jesus knew that a piece of the Divine had been placed in Mary, for when God breathed breath into the first parents, each successive human being was created in that holy image. Mary had found one who loved her tenderly, loved her sweetly, loved her intimately. And she was going to get to him, no matter what it took.

So, early, while it was yet dark, Mary was searching. Not only was it twilight, silent and dismal on the horizon, it was twilight, silent and dismal inside Mary. There was a deep interior emptiness within her. She held inside herself a vast contemplation of longing and one deep abyss of sorrow. There was a hole in her soul. The only one who had accepted her, loved her, and valued

her humanness was dead. She wanted to say farewell to love.

I know how the girl felt. There have been many
difficult periods in my life. I've been hurt, been
disappointed, had great sorrow, lost loved ones,
cried, lamented, and been disturbed by the actions of so-called friends. I've been lied to, talked
about, plotted against, and betrayed. And I have
looked for the Lover of my soul. Often I have
felt, like Mary, that "Jesus must be dead!" Can
you identify with her feelings too?

In your midnight experience, what do you do?
Most of us give up, turn around, and forget the
history that has brought us through. In the
dismal periods, we stay home, pull away from
community, and remain silent about our pain.
In the bad times, we say we don't want to trouble
anybody else with our sorrows. In actuality, we
are ashamed and feel like failures, and we
don't want anyone else to see us at less than our
best. "When I get it all together, I'll come back
to church." "When I get up on my feet, I'll get
active again." "When I get over this hump, then
I'll seek Jesus."

The lesson Mary teaches us is that it's when
things are worst that we need to seek Jesus. While
the grief is fresh and the disappointment is real,

you need to get up and get out. Oleta Adams sings to remind us that if you have to come by caravan, by rail, by van, or by bus, get to Jesus any way you can! Don't wait, don't delay, don't put it off; remember to seek Jesus. We need to surround ourselves with every type of high-praise worship experience during the good times, for every good time is a reminder that midnight is coming.

Now, Mary knew that a great stone would block her entrance to the one she sought. But she pressed on anyway. Even four strong people could not have moved that stone, for tombs were hewn out of rocks almost four feet high. Mary knew she would need some additional help. She knew that her resources were limited. She knew that this was not a job for one person to do alone. But she was willing to take the journey and to leave the stone to be dealt with when she got there. God had already moved the stone out of her way!

Who would you be if Christ moved the stone in your life? The Bible doesn't tell us how the stone got moved, for every "stone" gets moved in a different way. God has a miracle with your name on it when you decide to seek Jesus in earnest. What if the broken hopes and shattered dreams of your life were woven back together and new pieces of beauty began to appear upon your horizon; who would you be? If the pain and unforgivingness over a broken relationship were healed and your heart could feel glimmers of hope, who would you be? Suppose the desire for alcohol and drugs would simply disappear; who would you be? Imagine that the tears, the grief, and the anguish over a loss faded into the background, and new life came in surprising ways; who would you be?

Mary didn't know who she would be. She knew only who she had been, one who was lost and out of community. She knew what she had become because of the love of Jesus; she had become a woman of hope and possibilities. She knew how something within had changed and how hope had come into her life. She knew that what was had come to an end on the cross, and she had no idea who she would be now. Friend of mine, when Jesus is absent from our lives, there's no telling who we will be, what we will do, or where we will end up. When Jesus is absent, our lives are dismal and we are on a constant search for meaning, validation, and assurance. When Jesus is absent, we will do anybody and anything, seeking a substitute. There is no friend like Jesus!

Mary the bodacious woman ran and got the

two best friends of Jesus, and they came back to the tomb with her. They believed that Jesus' body had been stolen, for scripture records that "as yet they did not understand the scripture, that he must rise from the dead" (John 20:9). They returned to their homes and left Mary in the grave-yard. Wake up, beloveds! You can't get help from just anyone. You can't accept the advice of just anyone. You can't expect just anyone to stand by you. Sometimes you simply have to stand alone. When Jesus' friends went back to the confines of their locked houses, girlfriend stood outside the tomb weeping over the loss of the body of Jesus.

Some of us think that crying will fix a problem. Some of us think that a good cry is the answer. Some of us are good at pitiful crying. But as Mary cried, she continued moving. Your tears of self-pity cannot immobilize you. Your tears of sadness cannot make you paralyzed. Your tears of humiliation, guilt, and shame cannot hinder you so severely that you can't see the other options available in a given situation. As Mary cried and bent over, she saw the angels that Jesus' friends had missed. As she cried and knelt, she received words of comfort that the fellows who had run off had not received. In our greatest distress, God dispatches an angel on the run with a message of hope. Our loving God cries with us. Our faithful Creator hurts with us. Our infinite Lover longs to console us. Even as Mary cried, help was already there. And the question the angel asked is for each one of us in our immediate situation: "Woman, why are you weeping?" (John 20:13). She was looking for Jesus among the dead, but he was not there.

Looking for hope in things is not the answer. Looking for joy in people is not the answer. Looking for security in material possessions is not the answer. Looking for self-esteem in accomplishments is not the answer. The only answer is in Jesus Christ, who will not be found in dead things. But he is as close as you need, for Jesus called Mary by name.

The scripture says Mary thought Jesus was the gardener. This means that they were in the Garden of Gethsemane. She had come to the garden alone, while the dew was still on the roses.[2] And the joy she found was better than what she expected. This second Adam came to overturn "the fall" of women in the first garden experience. In this garden, the curse was lifted from women. In this garden, the wrong was made right. In this garden, a woman was given the power, the authority, and the mandate to go and tell the message of salvation. In this place, because of her tenacity, the curse was reversed. For the second Adam, who had risen from the dead, whispered to Mary, who represented Eve, saying, "Remember! Remember! Mary, remember who you are. Mary, remember what you have become. Mary, remember the potential within you. Mary, remember the message of liberation, freedom, and salvation that I have taught. Go back and remind my brothers to remember!"

The message of Easter is that we always have to be on the alert for the Resurrected One who comes to call us by name. Easter says that in the worst times, there is a message of hope. Easter says that God still moves stones and allows us to enter places we dared not dream. Easter says that the light yet shines and that help is on the way. Easter says that death does not have the final word. Easter says that down is not out and away is not gone. Easter says that Friday, with cross bearing and torture, will come, but Sunday is on the way. Easter says that if I hold on, even with my pain, my hurt, and my tears, a word of comfort will come.

Easter says that Jesus healed the sick to show us his power over helplessness. Jesus walked on water to show us his power over Mother Nature. Jesus calmed the raging sea and told the winds to chill to show us his power over every element. Jesus touched little children to show us his love for the insignificant. Jesus gave messages to women to show his regard for the nonvalued. Jesus saved a dying thief to show us his compassion for the least and the worst. Jesus breathed out forgiveness to show us the power of healing love. Jesus died on a rugged cross to show us his power over death. And Jesus rose again to show us that if we remember, simply remember, then,

One glad morning when this life is over,
I'll fly away.
To that home, on God's celestial shore,
I'll fly away.
I'll fly away, oh glory
I'll fly away.
When I die, hallelujah, by and by
I'll fly away.
Just a few more weary days and then
I'll fly away
To that land where joy shall never end
I'll fly away.[3]

Jesus called Mary "Woman" the first time he spoke, and she didn't recognize him. The pain of loss and the confusion of identity caused her not to know her friend and teacher. I feel in my spirit that he wanted her to hear him say, "It's all right, bodacious woman," for the name "Woman" includes you and me. The name "Woman" pulls us into this significant story. The name "Woman" goes back to redeem and reclaim even Mother Eve. Then, Jesus called her by name, "Mary." There's something about the sound of your own specific name. Your reading this particular book says that you have heard Jesus calling your name. Now what will you do since Christ has called your name? How will you respond? For it's evident that Jesus wants you to become a bodacious woman!

Some of you will return to the old, searching ways of your past. You've read a book on self-help, paid your conscience's debt, and can't wait to get back to business as usual. Some of you will go back to the dead things in your life, desperately seeking satisfaction. But I pray that some of you will acknowledge Jesus' call and accept the challenge of the risen Savior. Others of you have already heard the call, and you have answered with your life. Now it's time to listen for the assignment Jesus has for you.

Mary was given a message and a mission: "Go and tell." How will you go and tell the world about this One who calls us to fly? How will you do ministry in the name of the One who ministers unto you? Will you get involved in the ministry of God's church? Will you give of your time, your talents, and your efforts to do something for those who are in need? Our babies need to hear about our ability to fly. Our teens need to hear about our ability to fly. Our young adults need to hear about our ability to fly. Our middle-aged ones need to hear about our ability to fly. Our elders need to hear about our ability to fly. Every one of us has an assignment. Listen. Hear Jesus call your name.

Jesus said, "Mary, don't hold on to me." Your salvation is not just for Sunday morning performances. Jesus says we have to get out of the buildings. Jesus says your salvation is both personal and corporate. Your salvation has to be both an interior relationship with God and one that reaches out into your community.

Mary went to tell the story. We need to leave our place of comfort today, ready to tell our brothers and sisters, "Remember! Remember! The people could fly!" And, bodacious woman, so can you!

Just Between Us

- What strong women can you remember from your history?
- What are your favorite stories of your female ancestors who not only survived but achieved?
- Are you named after any of the women in your past?
- What strengths of theirs are realized in you?
- When was the last time you tried to "fly"?
- Who are the sisters you can call when the "demons" attack you?
- Have you a support group to walk with you when your way is shadowed?
- How have you successfully handled periods of depression and defeat?
- Name the "stones" in your life that only God can move.
- Are you looking for life in "dead things" or "dead people"?
- Have you remembered lately that life lives in *you*?

Suggestions

Research the meaning behind your name. Remember that the power of naming was given to our First Mother. The attributes, the strengths, and the awesome qualities within you are in many ways connected to the woman (or women) for whom you were named. Claim those powers!

chapter four

Not Bent or Bowed

The Bent-over Woman

Luke 13:10–17

"Come on, come on, now! Sit up straight! Don't slouch! Get those shoulders back, and take that crook out of your neck!" How many times have we heard these admonitions from parents, teachers, and drill sergeants? Somewhere along the line, we have came to understand that good posture plays a positive role in how we feel and think about ourselves and how we portray ourselves to the world. No matter what community we live in, we all have the problem of seeing our youth walking around slumped over, wearing baggy clothes hanging off their waists. And we know that, essentially, the way they look indicates their poor concept of themselves and the negative ways they view the world and act toward each other and toward the adult population. We see them, and it's on the tip of our tongues to say to them, "Come on, come on, now, stand up straight! Get those clothes on correctly and be somebody!" For we really do believe that if you have good self-esteem, if you are a person of worth and dignity, and if you possess self-confidence, you will present yourself to the world properly erect, decently dressed, and with the correct decorum.

Today the call to sit up, stand up straight, get those shoulders back, and be erect and ready for what's at hand also comes to the church, straight from the mouth of the living God. For the church of God is slouching. The church of God has its head bent toward the ground, acting as if there are no answers to the problems going on in the world around it. The church of God is not standing erect nor behaving as if it believed it is a people of worth, dignity, and value. The church of God is stooped over, fighting about whether homosexuals should be ordained, while its members are wondering whether those already ordained ever hear a word from God!

The voice of God continues to echo through the ages, calling the church to stand up straight, get those shoulders back, stop slouching, and walk the talk. But the truth of the matter is that most of the members of the church are living lives of desperation. Most of us are simply trying to keep from going over the edge. If we dared to take an honest survey, we would be shocked and surprised at the number of church folks who are perpetually struggling with issues of depression, resentment, bitterness, and unforgivingness. We wonder why the young folks don't have good self-esteem; all we need to do is to look at our own lives!

The church is filled with people who are broken, fragmented, and hurting. We church members live empty lives, mouth empty, meaningless words to each other, and know that we have a hole in our souls that is aching to be filled. We want something. We search for something. We look for something and someone who will make us feel wanted, needed, and worthy. We look for something and someone who will bring satisfaction and meaning to our lives. We need something and someone who will make us feel authentic, real, and worthy. We are people who are bent over and bowed down—not always by the cares of the world, not always by the needs in our homes, not always by the situations in our jobs, but by the most active demon in the world. This demon, who is attacking and defeating the church of the living God, is the one who robs us of our self-esteem, steals our self-worth, and kills our confidence. The lack of self-esteem, confidence, and hope will make you bowed down and stooped over.

I submit to you that the problem of low self-esteem is the most crucial problem in the church today, for the issue of low self-esteem crops up whenever there is a hunger for dignity and respect in our lives. We are created in the image of the Divine. Each one of us is valued and cherished by God. Each one of us has a role to play, a gift to exercise, and a ministry to perform in the universal drama of life. But sin has entered and ruptured each one of our lives. Sin has its effects in the way we see ourselves and in the way we view each other. Rodney Dangerfield says it best when he rolls his eyes and says, "I just don't get no respect!"

When you don't get the respect you deserve, it prompts feelings of shame inside you. When you don't get the respect of parents, teachers, and peers, it causes an interior threat to your sense of security, and it breaks down your self-confidence. When you don't get the respect, the listening to, the attending to, and the care for, you begin to live in great fear. And the root of that fear comes from your value and dignity being threatened. We grow up thinking, believing, and saying, "I can't do this"—whatever it is—because we have not learned to master these ego-threatening situations. Shame, insecurity, self-negation, and self-hatred stem from being made to feel that you are not worthwhile. Shame, insecurity, self-negation, and self-hatred will make you walk bent over and bowed down. But the Word of God has some key lessons so that we might stand up straight, not slouch, and begin to act like the worthwhile, valuable people of God that we are.

In Luke 13:10–17, we find a sister who had been crippled by a spirit for eighteen years. She had a spirit of being bent and bowed. She was not physically ill, as we might immediately think, but the Bible says that a satanic spirit had taken up residence in her being. She was bent over and was quite unable to stand up straight. If our sister had a simple physical ailment, she would have been better off. But sister-girl had a spirit that had made itself at home in her. I know we don't want to talk about devils, evil spirits, demons, and the demonic, but when they appear in the Scriptures, we have to deal with their reality and see what Jesus has to say about them. This gives us a good opportunity to watch Jesus and a bodacious woman.

There are many spirits that can cause you to walk around in a bent-over state. They might be your color, your gender, your age, your marital state, your family; or they could be abuse, injustice, resentment, oppression, despair, loneliness, your economic state, or even a physical challenge. It makes no difference what has hurt you in the past, it makes no difference how old you were when the trauma affected your life, and it makes no difference what your wealth, position, or status is. For the evil one comes to steal, kill, and destroy, and each one of us is a candidate for being bent and bowed.

I want to make perfectly clear that it's normal to be bent over. The average person is bowed down with some affliction that impairs his or her ability to maneuver in life with head held high and shoulders straight. Social work statistics indicate that very few of us function wholly, which means that the majority of us are dysfunctional, bent over, and not able to stand erect. Get the message that the enemy of our lives will send a spirit to live at your house, one that will work on your job and, as with our sister, will make itself at home in *you*!

Some of us are full of the devil! Some of us have become emotionally, spiritually, and psychologically incapacitated. Some of us are miserable and make everybody around us crazy. Some of us have no sense of what it means to be whole, to be healed, or to be saved from the torture of evil spirits, for it is normal for the world to be bent over, bowed down, filled with despair, and singing the blues. But it is not normal for born-again, Holy Spirit-filled Christians. We are different. We have been made new creations. We have the ability to live a different reality. For Jesus has dealt with the demonic on our behalf. Are you ready to stop being bent over and bowed down? Do you really want to know how to get up? Realize that when you do know what to do, then you become responsible to straighten up and stand up and be the church of the living God.

It makes no difference to God whether you are afflicted by a spirit of inner poverty, which feels like a broken spirit, awful shame, or unbearable grief; or by a deserved guilt, suicidal depression, or spiritual weakness that kicks your backside. God wants you to know that you are delivered. You might have an inferiority complex and feel unlovable; or you might be afflicted with a murmuring, complaining, grumbling spirit because you don't like yourself and can't like anybody else. It's all right, for God is able to deal with you just where you are. Many are the people in your life who act as if they are sure of themselves, always confident and self-assured, but when you watch them carefully, you may find them always pulling down others simply because they too are unsure, uncertain, and filled with fear themselves. Even those who feel unworthy of being loved can find assurance in the Scriptures. For Jesus has come to address our needs. Jesus has come with a healing word. Jesus has come to say that we don't have to remain either bent over or bowed down.

Jesus did six things in the passage from Luke that allow us to lift up our heads. First of all, we understand that Jesus saw the woman in her bent-over condition. When others fail to see the pain we carry, Jesus takes notice of us. We have a God who cares about us so much that the hairs on our head are numbered. We have a God who told Jeremiah, "I knew you before you were born, and I had a plan for your life" (Jeremiah 1:5). This sort of intimate, caring, and concerned Creator sees our every move and wants to be involved in every aspect of our lives. There is no spot where God is not! Even when it is our fault that we are living in hell, God is there. God cannot take away

all of the painful situations in our lives, for sin is
the cause. Rebellion, disobedience, and defiance
by our original parents brought about this breach,
this separation and disconnection from God. But
God never moved from us. Jesus came with the
assurance that wherever you are, right where you
sit, you are not alone, for God is aware of what
you are going through and God cares for you.

Second, Jesus called the woman. "Softly and
tenderly, Jesus is calling, calling poor sinner come
home," says the songwriter.[1] When things are going their worst for you, stop, be still, and listen,
for the soft voice does not call over the loud
clamor and foolishness. But if you do as Howard
Thurman suggests and center down, you can hear
the gentle voice calling unto you. Remember:

I come to the garden alone
while the dew is still on the roses,
and the voice I hear falling on my ear,
the Son of God discloses.
And he walks with me, and he talks with me,
and he tells me I am his own;
and the joy we share as we tarry there,
none other has ever known.[2]

Jesus yet calls.

Third, Jesus spoke to the woman: "Woman,
you are set free from your ailment" (Luke 13:12).

It was the command of liberation. It was the breaking of the yoke. It was the falling away of the chains that had held her bound for eighteen long years. How long have you been tormented by demons? How long have you been imprisoned with a bowed spirit? How long has the enemy had the victory over your life? When you decide to get up, the chains have to turn you loose. For the Bible declares that those the Human One sets free are set free indeed. Liberation means new opportunity, unlimited potential, new beginnings. Forgetting all those things that have held us bound, we can look forward to what we can be in Jesus Christ.

The fourth thing Jesus did was touch the woman, lay hands on her, and immediately she stood up straight. The power of touch in the name of Jesus is awesome. This is why we reach out and touch each other in prayer. This is why we often lay hands on each other. For the ability to impart healing belongs to the church, and touching is the means by which we convey this restorative ministry of Jesus Christ. For anytime in the Scriptures that Jesus touched, healing was granted, restoration was guaranteed, and new power was received. And Jesus still touches those in need. Many are the ways you can be touched by Jesus.

Sometimes it is the tangible brush of air, wind, or breath that soothes and refreshes our spirits. More often it's the hand of a caring soul who reaches out with a card, a call, or assistance to lighten the load. At just the time you need it, there is a touch from God.

The fifth thing Jesus did is key for me. The church leaders had the audacity to become indignant because the woman was healed. This lets me know that everybody does not want to see you get well. There are people in the church, sitting right beside you, who want you to stay bound and bent over. And for sure the people in your home and on your job want you to stay just the way you are. For they know how to work your nerves, they know how to push your buttons, and they know what makes you tick. If you get well, what will they do? If you get well, who will be the fool in their midst? If you get well, who will they have to look down on and talk about? Jesus called the church leaders "hypocrites." He questioned them: "Ought not this woman, a daughter of Abraham whom Satan bound for eighteen long years, be set free from this bondage on the sabbath day?" (Luke 13:16).

Jesus said, "This is the church." The church is the healing station. The church is for the sick, the ill, the afflicted. There is a promise that deliverance belongs to the church. Look at Jeremiah 1:4–10. This prophet, this messenger, this awesome man of God told God that he could not perform the task before him, for he was hampered by his youth. All of us have some excuse for why we are hampered. But God does not accept our excuses. We can no longer point the finger at our past, our parents, or any other of our deficits.

For God said to Jeremiah, just as Jesus said to the woman and now says unto us today, "Do not be afraid of them, for I am with you to deliver you" (Jeremiah 1:8). This is the key; here is the answer! Right before us lies the antidote to being bent and bowed. It's knowing without a shadow of a doubt that God is with me and that I have no need to fear: "Greater is he that is in me than he that is in the world" (1 John 4:4). When God is with me, "I can do all things through Christ who strengthens me" (Philippians 4:13). For "he is able to do exceeding, abundantly above all I can ask or think, according to the power that works in me" today (Ephesians 3:20)! This is my self-esteem. This is my self-confidence. This is my blessed assurance—not who or what I am, but *whose* I am. I'm a child of God!

Finally, Jesus gave the woman a new name. He called her "Daughter." He acknowledged their relationship as blood kin. He reminded the church leaders that she was related to Abraham just as she was, and she had a right to every benefit of the covenant. For the covenant binds us to God, and all God has belongs to me. The covenant says that I am the righteousness of God in Christ Jesus. The covenant says that Jesus was bruised for my iniquities, that the punishment that brought us peace was upon him, and that by his stripes I am already healed. The covenant says that when Jesus died on Calvary, he died for me. When Jesus rose, my eternal life was guaranteed. His death says that I don't have to be bent or bowed. His death says that I can be set free from the demonic that seeks to destroy me. His death says, "Victory is mine!"

Did you notice that all the bent-over woman had to do was be in God's house and her healing took place? All of the initiative was on the part of Jesus. Jesus does not want us bent over or bowed down. Jesus sees the needs of your life. Today is your day for healing. The woman was immediately set free. You can be different, changed, and unlike before. All the woman had to do was give God praise, and the church began to rejoice with

her. Today, as you offer unto God yourself and
your gifts, the Holy Spirit is ready and waiting to
anoint you, to lay hands on you, and to touch
your life that you might go forth in victory, not
bent and not bowed.

One day, I came to Jesus just as I was, weary,
worn, and sad, for the abuse of my childhood
had bent me over. The pain of rejection by those
who were my primary caregivers had my head
and my heart bowed in shame. The inner gloom
of my spirit had caused many love relationships
to go wrong, and other relationships had never
been loving. For the evil spirit of shame had a
home in my spirit, and I had been afflicted since
my childhood. I didn't want a relationship with
a male God who might abuse me, take advantage of me, and cause me more pain. So for years
I ran from the house of God. For many years, I
tried to find things and people to satisfy the hunger and emptiness in my soul. Yet the Holy Spirit
never gave up on me.

One Sunday morning, having taken my sons
to church school and remaining to take them
home after worship, the Holy Spirit arrested my
attention. I heard the voice of God speaking
through the sermon. The hand of Jesus touched

me, freed me, and the healing process began in
my life. I found in Jesus a resting place, and this
bodacious woman has been standing up and
moving forward ever since!

Just Between Us

- Have you been bent over lately?
  Can you identify what's got you stooped?
- How many times in the last week have you
  responded, "I can't do that"? Have you read
  any books on self-esteem in the last month
  or so?
- Do you understand that the woman in Luke
  13:10–17 was afflicted with a spirit?
- Do you understand that Jesus really does
  see and care about you?
- Has the reality hit home that you too can
  be made well?
- Is there some significant individual in your
  life who does not want you well and
  standing up straight?
- Have you heard Jesus calling to you
  "softly, tenderly"?
- What will liberation from stooping look
  like for you?
- How will you be different? the same?

Suggestions

Find some scriptural affirmations, type them in bold print, and tape them to the mirror, the refrigerator, the dashboard, your desk, and other places you look at often. Repeat them over and over to yourself until they become a part of you. This will change the negative thought patterns of your mind. Recall the hymn or praise song that motivates and moves you when you hear it on Sunday. Buy a recording of it and play it on the way to work, as you walk or jog, and before you go to bed. Singing is another way to change your thoughts, your behaviors, and your life!

chapter five

AN EXECUTIVE DECISION
TIME TO GET UP

Isaiah 53

Have you ever asked yourself the question "What am I doing here?"[1] When around you others seem to be moving forward, accomplishing, achieving, and pushing ahead, have you ever wondered why you did not make the progress that you wanted, planned, and strategized to make? "What am I doing here?" is a reality-facing question. It's an existential problem that surfaces whenever we begin to challenge our presence in a situation or circumstance. It becomes a prayer: "God, help me understand what I am still doing here." It's a petition for comprehension of the problem. It's a plea for the grace to move out of this location. It expresses a persistent need for divine intervention to assist you in getting up and moving on.

I know from personal experience that sometimes the dilemmas in our lives have been so overwhelmingly powerful that our only response is to sit. Have you ever had to deal with unexpected calamities, unforeseen disappointments, messed-up plans, delayed dreams, unrealized visions, dashed hopes, unfulfilled goals, unwelcome visitations of negative forces, love affairs gone wrong, and adult children who won't stay gone? Any one of these surprise attacks by the enemy of our souls can cause us to stagnate, vegetate, ruminate, and just plain sit.

We sit and try to figure out how to move, but we can't. We sit and try to muster up some strength, but we can't. We sit and want to ask somebody for help, but we don't. We sit and begin to get analytical about why we can't move. We sit. We sit and blame others for our situation and decide that it really isn't our fault that we don't move. So we don't. We sit. We sit and wait for someone to come and get us up, but no one comes. So we sit. We say that we are waiting for the right time to come, but it never does. So we sit.

Our inability to get up, get started, and finish what we start is legendary as we recall our many partially read books that we never finished. There are volumes of letters and notes that we thought of writing but never even began. There are hundreds of diets that we start but quit before we realize our goal. Do you have any half-finished item in your sewing basket or any well-planned work project that you just can't seem to get around to? We have good intentions, but we get stuck. So we sit. I am persuaded that each one of us is in one of three cycles of life. You just got out of some difficult spot, or you are in the middle of a difficult spot, or a difficult spot is on its way to your house! For we are stormy weather people, and the blues hang around all the time. But Jesus has come to say that it's time to get up. It's time to move ahead with your life. It's time for you to make an executive decision to be a bodacious woman.

The movie *Executive Decision* is about a foreign terrorist group that takes a plane of American citizens hostage and threatens the security of the entire East Coast. What is the president to do to resolve this diplomatic crisis and save the lives of his people? It sounds just like the devil's plot in the Garden of Eden to me. For Satan was determined to hold us in slavery to sin. But thank God that an executive decision had already been enacted in Jesus Christ.

The Scriptures declare that "the thief comes to do only three things in our life: to steal, to kill, and to destroy" (John 10:10). It ought not be so surprising when things go wrong, because they often will. But we act as if trouble is some new feature on earth. And instead of moving forward, we sit. It's all right to sit on things, but this sitting attitude has painfully invaded too many vital areas of our lives. Mothers are sitting while children are being neglected. Fathers are sitting while children are being abandoned. Churches are sitting cold, dead, and on the verge of meaninglessness while we sit on our faith and argue about how to reduce spending. Marriages are being wrecked while we sit. Dreams are being unrealized while we sit. A world is not being evangelized while we sit. Our children are being lost and our own souls are in dire jeopardy while we sit.

So, it's essential that we stop and ask ourselves, "What am I doing here?" I'm struggling with the same issues, wrestling with the same problems. I'm yet dissatisfied with my self-image. I'm still unfulfilled in my marriage. I'm still depressed about being single. I'm still grappling with the surges and urges of my sexuality. I still can't forgive that one person, and I refuse even to speak to that other one. So I'm physically here, but in my spirit I'm just going to sit!

Well, sisters, resurrection is about new life. Resurrection is about getting up and being different. Resurrection is about change, transformation, and movement. Our sitting is an affront to the God of the Resurrection. Our sitting is an insult to Jesus. For our sitting says that we don't trust God enough to believe that anything can be done about our particular situation. It's an insult to God because we are saying that God does not have the power, the ability, or the authority to change our lives. To sit and do nothing is a blatant demonstration of faithlessness. To sit and not be fulfilled is to live beneath your inheritance as a child of the Most High. To sit is to invalidate the life, suffering, and cruel death of Jesus. To sit is to say that God's week ends on Friday and that Sunday will never come. To sit is to make the Resurrection a fairy tale starring Jesus as the Easter bunny.

So, I say that it's time for you to make an executive decision. It's time for you to make some quality management determinations about your life, your lifestyle, and your choice of a god. For the God I serve made an executive decision concerning us even before the world began. Before there was a when or a where, before there was a now or a then, Jesus had made the executive decision to be born in our skin; to walk in our shoes; to suffer our pains; to be rejected, abandoned, and misunderstood; to go about doing good while being talked about, lied on, vilified, and even crucified for you and me.

I'm so glad that Jesus didn't decide just to sit. When the devil came and tempted him in the wilderness, the confusion of his many choices of approach to ministry could have made him sit. When he saw that his disciples were unlettered, smelly, and fearful fishermen, the complexity of companionship could have made him sit. When his teaching seminars brought dumb questions and blank looks, when his miracles were not wanted in his hometown, and when the people followed him only for the loaves and fishes, the painful reality of seeming failure could have made him sit.

If we use troubles as an excuse to sit, Jesus had them. If we use heartaches as an excuse to sit, he had them. If we use crazy family members as an excuse to sit, he had them. If we use the strange and bizarre behaviors of church members to sit, he had them. If we use the lack of financial resources to sit, he had that too: he didn't have a steady job, depended upon the resources and alms of wealthy women, and was homeless for more than three years. So no excuse is acceptable from us, for he lived in our shoes; he experienced our frustrations and agony; his companions abandoned him in his most needful hours; and his most comprehending student, Mary, the sister of Lazarus, didn't even understand that he could be four days late and still be right on time, so he even shed our tears. But he did not sit! For he had made an executive decision to die in our stead that we might live abundantly and eternally.

Life is rough, but we can get up. We will have many painful setbacks, but we can get up. It seems as if the world is crumbling around our feet, but we can get up. Many folks have walked off and left us to carry on the battle alone, but we can get up. We have had enough time to wallow in self-pity. It's time to wipe your weeping eyes and put your hands on your hips and the Word of God on your lips. For we have got to make that executive decision to get up and get busy.

The plan of getting up was prophesied by the prophet Isaiah thousands of years ago. He told us that Jesus would not find a kind reception awaiting him. He informed us that the gospel would not be well received. He outlined how few would believe the report of Jesus and that not many would embrace this new paradigm for living. Isaiah told us that there would be a great rebellion against this One born in North Galilee. The Messiah was not supposed to come out of some little poor family, from a region that was of such ill repute that nothing good could come from it. Galilee was desert; there could be no green, lush, valuable life born there, only roots shooting up out of dry ground.

Jesus didn't come looking like an exceedingly fair Moses the Deliverer. Nor did he come as a charming and melodious King David, for there was nothing appealing about his looks. And his words were too plain. He didn't have an education from the school of the rabbis, and he had no social credentials to pull the right folks to him. He was acquainted with grief and familiar with sorrows, for rejection by your own folks is pain of the greatest sort. Being a man of color born into impoverished economic conditions and living with fair-weather folks, he knew grief as an intimate acquaintance. Yet he took on the misery he knew we would have to bear. He sympathized with you and me so much that he left the beauty, the splendor, and the reverence of heaven, stepped on the down escalator in glory, and came to endure the contradictions of humankind. Thank God that he didn't come to sit!

The executive decision had been made when he told God to prepare him a body and to allow him to come down to redeem, recover, and reclaim fallen humanity. This executive decision had the weight of heaven behind it, the authority of the eternal around it, and the power of resurrection within it. When the world turned its back on him, his executive decision held him steady. When his friends betrayed him and ran away in the cover of night, his executive decision helped him tell God, "Nevertheless, not my will . . ." When his own people marked him a bad man and allowed a known criminal to be set free in exchange, his executive decision carried him from judgment hall to judgment hall. When the people lied on him, spat on him, and mocked him with a crown of thorns, it was his executive decision that put determination in his eyes and strength in his will, and helped him decide not to call ten thousand angels.

The executive decision led him to a garbage dump called Golgotha, where the people laid him upon an old rugged tree. They nailed spikes in his ankles and wrist bones to secure him to

Calvary's tree. They lifted him high and mocked him to come down. They gambled for his clothes and offered him vinegar to drink. But through it all he didn't sit down on his executive decision. For the executive decision was to die in my place. The executive decision was to go to hell for me. The executive decision was to beg my pardon with God for the sin that is born in me. The executive decision was to heal my wounded spirit and to mend my broken heart. The executive decision was to allow him to be stricken, smitten of God, forsaken by his divine parent in my place. If he wouldn't sit down on me, how can I sit down on him?

Jesus was oppressed and afflicted for me. He offered himself as the perfect sacrifice, not for popular opinion and personal acclaim but for me. With his wisdom he could have evaded the sentence of death. By his divine power he could have resisted this ignominious execution. But the executive decision had been made, and therefore he stuck with the resolution of the cross. As a sheep he was led to the slaughter, and as a lamb he didn't open his mouth.

He hung there and declared his mission was complete. "It is finished!" He hung there and welcomed me. "Today, you will be with me in Paradise!" He hung there and made sure I could have community. "Woman, behold your son. Son, behold your mother." He hung there and mandated my getting up, because he wouldn't come down. He hung there and put power in my hands by allowing them to take the power out of his. He hung there and negated the spirit of sitting, whining, and complaining, for he never said a mumbling word. He hung there until I got the message that sitting down on God is not the answer. He hung there until my own executive decision could be fixed in my spirit. "Oh, God, into your hands I commit my spirit!" (Luke 23:46). I give myself away—it's the least that I can do! "I surrender all. All to thee, my blessed Savior, I surrender all!"[2]

His hanging there in my stead demands an executive decision on my part. His perfect sacrifice for my salvation dictates a response from me. His offering of himself for my transgressions directs me to reply to this love divine. "Some folks would rather have houses and land. Some folks chose silver and gold. These things they treasure and forget about their souls."[3] But I've made an executive decision, I've decided no more sitting down, I've committed to standing up for the right. I've just decided to make Jesus Christ my choice!

Just Between Us

- Do you "plan your work and work your plans"? Or are you one who reacts?
- Are you indecisive, fickle, uncertain?
- Are you stuck?
- Have you been here before?
- Are you tired?
- Are you sick and tired of being sick and tired?

Suggestions

Do something! Take risks! Make mistakes! Learn from them! Move it, girl! Make executive decisions!

chapter six

❧

Pregnant with the Promise
Mary's Testimony

Luke 1:26–55

Mary had a little lamb, a little lamb, a little lamb,
oh, Mary had a little lamb and Jesus was his name.
He was born in Bethlehem
the Son of God by name,
miracles he came to do
to save me and you.
He died but then he rose again,
our sins he did redeem,
he's coming back again so soon
the Church of God to claim.

There is a troubling in my soul. There is a restlessness in my spirit. There is a disquieting rumbling within me. For it is almost time; I am fast approaching my time of birthing. For the Advent season is just the rehearsal for the coming of my little lamb. Friends of mine, Advent really means that the whole world is pregnant! It is pregnant with hope, pregnant with anticipation, pregnant with the expectation that something will be born that will make things different, better, changed. So the sighs that you hear, the moans that escape closed lips, and the heaviness you experience are simply the signs of a birth about to take place. But I'm moving too fast. Let me introduce myself. My name is Mary.

My story begins with an angel. Can you imagine what it's like to be awakened from a sound sleep by a strange voice speaking to you? I couldn't decide whether to be afraid, impressed, or just plain angry. How dare this being come into my sleeping space and scare me half to death, and then declare that I was blessed! For you know that the angel said, "Hello, Mary, you are filled with grace. You are blessed among women." I was filled with grace? What did this mean? Was grace something that I could taste, wear, or see? Was grace something that I could touch, handle, or measure? I was filled with grace?

I tell you that right then I was filled with many things, but I couldn't put my finger on the grace. I was filled with wonder. I was filled with the mystery of the moment. I was filled with speculation as to what was happening. I was filled with awe that perhaps I was fully awake and that this was really happening. For we had all heard that the Messiah was coming. We had all been assured of the promises. We had listened and nodded our heads in agreement. But for 450 years God had been silent. For 450 years God had not spoken. For 450 years God had seemed to withdraw from relationship with us. So what could this greeting mean for me and my life? What was this grace?

When I could hear, Gabriel explained that grace was God's plan for my life. Grace was the role I was to play in bringing forth God's divine promise of a Savior. I was to be filled with grace by the power of the Holy Spirit. Hmm, me, abundant and overflowing with grace? And, another question was, would I agree to participate in salvation's history and redemption's story?

Ah, sweet mystery of life! Here was an angel from the heavenly realm, speaking to me, a mere earthbound individual, asking if the Timeless One could be confined in my time-bound womb. Here was the God of Creation asking to be created within my being. Here was the almighty God asking to reverse the power of the universe and to become helpless, dependent, needy, and inferior as my child. Here was the royal Ruler of all the dominions of the earth, asking to be carried by a low-born servant. Here was the one with no limits, asking to be confined for a nine-month period, within the limits of my womanly space. The paradox and the absurdity of the situation overwhelmed me, and I was stunned, to say the least.

Can you understand my dilemma? The hands that created the world and shaped the sun and the moon wanted me to hold and kiss them. The dynamism that formed the raging, living oceans and seas wanted me to wash it with a rag. The energy that spoke the mountains, the trees, the animals into being wanted to nurse at my breast. The intelligence that breathed breath into our first parents wanted me to teach it how to talk and walk. The mind that conceived the galaxies and the hemispheres wanted to call me "Mother." It was monumental and breathtaking. My heart began to pound, and I became filled not with grace but with overwhelming anxiety.

How dare the angel say that I was blessed among women? Do you realize that I was only fourteen, not married but only engaged? I was a virgin, but I was not stupid. I knew that the people in my village could count to nine. I knew that the penalty for having a child out of wed- lock was being stoned to death. Your Bible calls Joseph a just man, but I knew that he was just a man—and what man would believe this tale? What man would go along with this scheme? What man would want to raise, feed, and take care of a baby who was not his? And what man wants to wait for sex?

Talk about being in the middle of a crisis! Yet Gabriel said I was blessed. I was scared half to death. But before I could panic completely, I heard the words that brought comfort to my spirit: "Fear not, Mary, for you have found favor with God." People of God down through the ages had been told to "fear not." In at least sixty-four of the Hebrew lessons I had heard in Temple, this phrase meant that God was going to perform a miracle. It meant that God was going to do something spectacular. It meant that God was going to be involved in using a human vessel to change the course of history. And, of all people, God wanted to use me!

Out of all the people who could have been selected, God chose me. It was more than my heart could conceive. It was greater than any of the ideas for marriage and family that I had dreamed and planned for. God wanted me to play a part in changing the destiny of the world. When this thought penetrated my swirling brain, I asked Gabriel, "How can this be?" For I needed to know something of God's plan. I needed to understand what my role would be. I needed to know exactly what God was asking of me. The angel told me not to have fear, but I did.

Has God ever asked you to do something out of the ordinary? Have you been asked to do a thing that has never been done before? God might do the work, but you are the up-front person. People won't talk about God, they'll talk about you. The finger-pointing and the tongue wagging will be directed at you. I knew this was a fact, so I asked the angel one question: "Tell me, how can this be?"

I was told to just be still and let God do the work for the moment: "The Holy Spirit will come upon you, and the power of the Highest shall overshadow you. Therefore, the holy one which shall be born of you shall be called the Son of God." I got the message. The lightbulb came on. For just as the Spirit of Creation had overshadowed the old chaotic world and brought cosmos out of nothing, this same reproducing Spirit would impregnate me with the seed of God. I was simply to let go and let God. Oh, its an awesome thing to sit still and focus on the activity of God. It's a great thing to cultivate a passive spirit and let God do the work. I was not to jump over pews, go on a fast, or roll on the floor. I was told just to be still.

Like you, I wanted to do something. Like you, I thought, surely there must be more to it than this. Like you, I wanted to help God out, put in my effort, do my part. But God simply wanted my "yes." It's unreal that the God of heaven and earth waited on me to agree to be a part of this wonderful plan. God won't take advantage of us. God won't go against our wills. God won't insist that we cooperate. But God will wait on us.

Talk about being wrapped in the love of God! Talk about being enfolded in the arms of bliss! Talk about being caught up in rapture! God chose me. God chose *me*. Out of all who could have been selected, God chose me. The wonder, the awe, the amazement of it all was too powerful for me to bear alone, so I was instructed to go and visit with my cousin Elizabeth. There is no mention of my mother in Scripture, for she couldn't believe. If it was too much for me, I knew she wouldn't be able to make sense out of it. Elizabeth was another woman who was dealing with her own mystery and bewilderment. It was easier for us to make connections and to wrestle together with our dilemmas.

God calls us. God chooses us. God selects us

for the missions we are to perform in life. We can rebel against God, we can ignore God, or we can submit. I was a willing vessel. I was living for God. I was available. And I was willing to become pregnant with the promise.

When you meet those conditions, the Holy Spirit will impregnate you. It makes no difference that you are female, male, old, or young. God is yet seeking those who are willing to bear Jesus into their world. Meister Eckhart, a German theologian of the fourteenth century, asked himself the rhetorical question "What does God do all day?" and he answered himself, "God lies on a maternity bed, giving birth to thoughts, dreams and visions."

Have you ever had a brilliant idea pop into your mind, and you wonder, "Where did this come from?" It's one of the seeds of God, looking for a fertile place to take root and grow. On the seventh day of creation, God finished the work of creation and sat down. The work of continuing the creation of the world is left up to the creatures of God. God continues to supply within us visions of greatness, dreams of hope, and thoughts for better tomorrows. Most of us will abort the pregnancy: "I can't do that; what will people think?" "We've never done it this way before; it won't be accepted." "This is not a part of the established tradition and the status quo; it won't fit." But if you won't take a risk for God, if you can't take a leap of faith, what happens to the creation story?

I was chosen so that Christ, the hope of glory, could be formed in me. This is all that God is asking of you! Will you allow Christ to be formed in you? For each one of us, called by the name of God, is required to reproduce Jesus in the places we affect on the earth. My child never traveled more than thirty miles from Bethlehem. If each one of us could just affect the house, the block, the community that we live in, what a difference this world would see.

I was expectant. I became excited. And I waited for the overshadowing to come. It would surely come. It comes to those who are willing to cease their own efforts, to cultivate stillness, and to have confidence in God. Oh, the situations of my life were not ideal. I was too young, too single, and just about to become homeless. My good name was going to be tarnished, my reputation was going to be questioned, and my future was uncertain. Yet I said yes, for I realized that new life was going to be imparted to me. I caught the vision that I was going to be a part of an everlasting dominion. I got the message that, come what may, what I was willing to contribute to the realm of God was going to last throughout eternity. I was willing to risk with God. I was willing to take a chance on God. I was willing to go along with this risky business since I had faith in God.

I had no guarantees. I had no support group. I had no family to back me up. But the angel directed me to go and see Elizabeth. I had no bus, no Holiday Inns, no credit cards, and no angelic security squad, but I was to go off on a three-day-and-night journey across the wilderness to see Elizabeth? It was three days of walking and asking myself if I was crazy, three days of trying to make sense of what I had gotten myself into, three days of tears, screams, and frustration. For I had no further information. I had no additional pledge, vow, or covenant. But I was pregnant with a promise.

I was full of the hope of the world. I was saturated with the Word of the living God. I was anticipating the Child who would come and bring peace to a troubled world. I was expecting the Alpha and the Omega, the beginning and the end of all the dominions of this world. And I was determined to go through! Oh, I had to sing to myself on the journey. I had to encourage myself as I walked along. I had to uplift my own spirits, for I felt so all alone. I told myself, "I'm going through. I'm going through. I'll pay the price, whatever others do. I'll take the way, with the Lord's despised few. I have started with Jesus, and I'm going through." I was bodacious!

I made it to Elizabeth's. It was intimidating to walk up to her home. Her husband, Zechariah, was a priest. Would he allow me to stay with them? Explaining my pregnancy wasn't going to be easy, for with the human mind this story doesn't add up. It takes great faith to believe that what God has promised, God will do. But who can believe it, when God has been silent for 450 years? Yet I should have known that God takes care of the minor details when we submit our wills in order to do God's work. When I arrived, it was Elizabeth who met me, and she was the prophet in the family!

Elizabeth was six months pregnant. But she came running to meet me. As she got close, she stopped and began to exclaim, "What does this mean that the mother of my Lord has come to visit me?" And when she said those words, a change came over her. She was filled with the Holy Spirit. The first person to be filled with the power of the living God was the woman who affirmed my being pregnant with the promise! If you don't want to do the unusual, if you aren't willing to be the one who lives on the edge, if you want to be among the careful and the cautious, you at least ought to be willing to affirm the one who will be a risk taker. You can stroke and promote and push that person. For you never know what God will do for you when you simply advocate for the promise that is to come.

Elizabeth's affirmation allowed my spirit to be at ease. I knew that God was truly in the plan. Yes, I had heard from an angel, but that could have been my imagination. I felt that I had seen him and heard him and talked with him, yet I had no eyewitness. Nobody could testify to my sanctity. But when Elizabeth prophesied, my heart begin to lift. When Elizabeth began to shout out the role I was to play in history without my saying a word, my soul begin to magnify God. My spirit began to rejoice in God, my Savior. For the One who was mighty had done great things to me!

Talk about a reversal of history! Talk about an upset to the status quo! Talk about a turnaround for the norms of our society! God's coming as a human; God's choosing a woman to be essential in the drama of new life; God's not waiting for

my marriage but choosing to use my status as
single, female, and young; God's using the least
to bring about the best; God's using the young
to bring into being the eternal; God's using a vessel to hold the uncontainable—God's mystery is
overwhelming. God's astonishment is baffling.
God's decision to use the ordinary to do the ex-
traordinary is so like God:

> God uses ordinary people. People just like
> you and me. People who are willing to do
> God's will. People who will give their all,
> no matter how small their all might be.
> For little becomes much when you place
> it in the Master's hand. Just like the little
> lad who gave Jesus all he had and the
> multitudes were fed with the fish and the
> loaves of bread. What you have may not
> be much, but when you yield it to the
> touch of the Master's loving hand, then
> you'll understand, and your life will never
> be the same. Ordinary people . . . God
> uses ordinary people.[1]

Let God use you today. Say: Yes, I'll be pregnant with the promise. Yes, I'll be a bodacious
woman. I'll carry Jesus everywhere I go. I'll bear

Jesus in my home. I'll take Jesus on my job. I'll carry Jesus to school. I'll give birth to Jesus in my life. I'll bring Jesus into my social settings. I'll let Jesus explode into my every plan and activity. I'll say, "Yes, Lord, yes, to your will and to your way. I'll say, yes, Lord, yes, I will trust you and obey. When your Spirit speaks to me, with my whole heart, I will agree, and my answer will be yes, Lord, yes!"[2]

Just Between Us

- What was the most recent "infant" you birthed into the realm of God?
- Who was there to help you with your labor?
- Name the significant woman you can share your "pregnancy" with.
- Have you been "midwife" for another sister's pregnancy?
- What sister's recent "baby" has been a blessing to your life?
- Is the local congregation you attend a safe place to give birth to the new?
- Isn't it wonderful to know that age, marital status, and economic limitations don't affect your being impregnated by the Holy Spirit?

Suggestions

What are your secret yearnings, hopes, and dreams? Get a journal and let them come to life on paper. Hold them close to your heart and nurture them. When you are ready, find a woman who is a risk taker to share them with. Remember that pregnancy is a long haul. Remember that some pregnancies end in miscarriage and spontaneous abortions. That's all right. You will get pregnant again!

chapter seven

≈

WE DRINK FROM THE WELL
THE WOMAN AT THE WELL

John 4

Early one Saturday morning in March, I finished ghostwriting a book for a black mother who kept a journal of her youngest son's two-year struggle with AIDS. It was one of the saddest stories I have ever read. Four months after this woman discovered that her big, fine, college-educated Marine Corps officer son was a homosexual, he told her that he was HIV-positive. He swore her to secrecy. She had two daughters and another son, yet she could not confide in her family. Her eighty-five-year-old dad was alive and was coming to live with her, but she couldn't tell him either. She had a sister and a brother, but the secret was hers to bear alone. In a year's time, her son had full-blown AIDS and every complication that accompanies it.

She ran an agency with a budget of more than $3 million and people reported to her, but she had no one to lean on. She belonged to one of the biggest churches in town and served on the most prestigious boards, but no one could see her pain. The pressure mounted, the bills increased, her son's health declined, yet she walked alone. She went to church Sunday after Sunday, waiting, hoping, searching for someone to notice, to reach out, to care. But she came home empty. For in the comfortable church with the cushioned pews, the people were spiritually asleep. In the place where songs of Zion are sung and sermons of victory are preached, the eyes of the church folks were closed and their ears could not hear her and her son's cries of desperation.

It's a sad story. There is no surprising, happy ending. Her son suffered and died. Three months later, her aunt died. Three months after that, her dad died. How did she survive? How could she cope? From what wells did she stop and drink? "Fill my cup Lord. I lift it up, Lord. Come and quench this thirsting of my soul. Bread of heaven, feed me till I want no more. Fill my cup. I lift it up. Come, make me whole."[1]

I don't like the New Revised Standard Version of the passage about the woman at the well. Whereas John 4:4 in the NRSV reads, "But he had to go through Samaria," the old King James and even the new King James Version has, "And Jesus had a need to go to Samaria." It makes a difference if Jesus had a need, a compulsion, to go and see a Samaritan woman. It's not an accident, a coincidence, or a casual mishap that Jesus happened upon the woman at the well; it's a deliberate, intentional, and calculated decision on the part of the Savior of the world to go to Samaria and meet with her.

It was about noon. In Near Eastern countries, the custom at noon is to siesta. At noon, the sun has reached its zenith. Noon is the hottest time of the day. At noon, most people try to be sheltered from the heat of the sun. But the Bible is clear that this meeting took place about noon. We all know the story of Nicodemus, slipping and tipping, trying to see Jesus in the night. But here we find Jesus trying to keep a date with a woman at high noon. For it was a hot time in her life. Most likely she felt that things couldn't get any hotter than they were. When the mother got the news that her son was homosexual, it got hot. But when she heard he was HIV-positive, it got hotter still. When she thought it was already boiling, along came full-blown AIDS. But we have a record of Jesus' habit of coming to meet women in the hottest time of their lives.

Is your husband not treating you right? It's hot. Want a husband and can't find one? It's hot. Got a husband and he ain't a husband? It's hot. Your kid's acting like a fool? It's hot. Want a baby and can't have one? It's hot. Hitting your head against the glass ceiling? It's hot. Can't find the job that will pay you what you're worth? It's hot. Got a secret and can't tell nobody? It's hot. Somebody spreading vicious lies all over town about you? It's hot. Somebody said that tea bags are at their best in hot water. But Girlfriend, you ain't no bag of tea, and hot water ain't comfortable! But there is hope. For Jesus had a need to go meet a woman, and he arrived when it was hot.

When it was the hottest part of the day, along came Jesus, and he asked the woman to do him a favor: "Give me a drink of water." Reciprocity is a universal principle. "Give and it shall be given unto you" (Luke 6:38). "You will reap what you sow" (Galatians 6:7). Jesus wanted to do something for this woman who was in hot water, so he asked her to do something for him. "Give to me in order that I might repay you in greater measure" was his bottom line. But Sister wanted to engage in cultural payback: "How is it that you, a Jew, ask a drink of me, a woman of Samaria?" (John 3:9). She had been taught from earliest childhood that the Jews and the Samaritans didn't mix. Jews looked down on Samaritans. Jews called them dogs, mongrels, half-breeds, for Samaritans were Jews who had intermarried with foreigners centuries before and had diluted their "pure" bloodline. A Jew would walk many extra miles to prevent passing by anything of a Samaritan's, and surely one would not walk through a Samaritan town.

So the woman's first reaction was one of shock that a Jewish man was asking her for a drink. Jesus said that the water he has in exchange was a gift from God (John 4:10). It is living water that will spring up inside of us to renew us, refresh us, revive us, and slake our inner thirst. When the woman comprehended, she asked to receive this gift, which was Jesus himself.

Then Jesus decided to address her hot issue. We have forty-two verses of scripture, which is the longest portion of dialogue between Jesus and any other one person in all of the Gospels. Just three verses, 16–18, deal with the woman's six "husbands." "Look, woman, you have had five husbands." Let's stop right here. This was not written last year or during the last twenty years. This was written almost two thousand years ago when women were simply the property of their fathers until they were given over to be the property of their husbands. There was no courtship and choosing of a mate. The marriage makers made the selection and helped establish the bride's price, and the marriage was consummated, like it or not. If the husband was dissatisfied over the sex, over the food, over the way his wife served his meals, he would go to the elders, state his argument, and get their decision to return to his tent, face the east, and declare three times, "I divorce thee, I divorce thee, I divorce thee." The woman took whatever he permitted and returned to her father's house as soiled goods. Five times Girlfriend had been bought and paid for, and five times she had been rejected. Was she in hot water or not?

Have you ever been rejected? ever been deserted? ever been abandoned, dropped, kicked to the curb, and dissed? If it's been done to you one time, how do you think the woman felt after it happened five times? What was the size of the hole in her soul? How big was the gaping wound forged there by uncaring, unkind, and insensitive men? This woman had been wounded. This woman was in pain. This woman was hurt. And Jesus went on to make it worse before it could get better.

Jesus says in verse 18, "And the one you have now is not your husband." This does not say that the woman is messing around, has loose morals, and is a cheap slut. It says that the one she is with today, number six, is just like the other five. He is not going to companion her, befriend her, or be a loving spouse to her. He is not the one, Girl! Heartache is on the way to her house again!

Many of us can truly identify with this woman. You may have gone from man to man, from relationship to relationship, and although the names changed, the story line remained the same. You give and give and get nothing but hurt in return. Some of you came from dysfunctional homes with dysfunctional parents, and you married a man just like dear old Dad. So you divorced the first one and married him again in the second one. For you have not changed. You keep attracting the same type of loser. Your antenna signals wrongdoers, users, and other idiots to come and whip game on you. But Jesus has a need to stop by your place today, for you are in hot water and about to step into a boiling pot!

Jesus helped Sister take a good look at herself. Jesus touched her in the raw, open, festering place where her pain resided. Jesus did not bypass the mess that was killing her self-esteem, ruining her self-confidence, and destroying her self-respect. You can't run away from the hurting in you. You can't run away from the pain in you. You can't outdistance the wound in you. It goes where you go and aches whether you deal with it or not. Jesus says, "Look, Girl, at what's destroying you. Look, Girl, at what's consuming your energies and dissipating your inspiration. Look, Girl, it's time for you to make a change." And Sister, it ain't about changing men. It ain't about changing jobs, apartments, or careers. It ain't even about changing hairstyles, dress colors, or fashion designers. It's about making a change in the inner you. It's about stopping and paying attention to the person you have become. It's about stopping to reflect upon the people you allow into the center of your stage. It's your video, your world. You ought to make conscious decisions about who will or won't have a starring part. Jesus came into your Samaria to keep a date with you, in the hottest part of *your* day, to say, "Girlfriend, let's work on *you*!"

Jesus told the woman to let God have center

stage: "God is spirit, and they who worship God will do it in spirit and in truth" (John 4:24). Sister, it's time to change your perspective. It's time to stop running to all the same wells, looking for something to satisfy you. It's time to stop staying away from the companionship of other women, who just might be able to help you see the mistakes you are making. It's time to search for genuine community where you can offer to other sisters some of the hard lessons you have learned. It's time to realize just how important you are to God, who loved you enough to send Jesus to meet you where you are. It's time for you to make a commitment to serve the living God. It's time for you to allow God to address that wounded, hurting, aching place within you that drives you to make foolish choices and irrational decisions.

For what you want is somebody to make you feel good about yourself. You want somebody who will accept you for who you are. You want somebody who will care about your needs and help you make it when the whole world runs out. You want a friend. You want a companion. You want a partner. "There is not a friend like the lowly Jesus, no, not one! No one can heal all your heart's diseases, no, not one. No, not one. For Jesus knows all about your troubles. He will guide till the day is done. There is not a friend like the lowly Jesus. No, not one. Oh, no, not one!"[2]

God is here today to keep a long-standing date with you. God is waiting by that old well that you have sipped from for so long, saying, "Look, Girl, there is some better, life-saving water for you." When Jesus comes into your life, you will know love and acceptance. When Jesus comes, you will know care and companionship. When Jesus comes, there will be healing from yesterday's pains, there will be forgiveness for yesterday's sins, and there will be satisfaction from yesterday's searching and drinking from the wrong wells. When you stop to let Jesus refresh you with the living waters of life, then you can come to love yourself. When you love yourself, your standards change. When your standards change, your attitude changes. And when your attitude changes, your antenna attracts a different type of person into your world. Now you have become a bodacious woman for Jesus!

Hanging on the old rugged cross, I can hear Jesus call out to his mother, "Look, Girl, you can't afford to be in this cruel world all by yourself. You've got to look further than me, your earthly son, and see God, who loved you enough to send me to meet your every need. Woman, stop grieving over this dying body, and realize that I have come to give you and all of your sisters in this old world new life, more abundant life, and life for all eternity. This world is not my home, I'm just passing through. You can have another son, but I'm the only Savior." Jesus kept his date with death so that we might live again. He kept his date with that woman by an old familiar well in the hottest part of the day so that you would know how much he loves you and me. He died so that he could come and see about that mother whose son died of AIDS. He died so that AIDS wouldn't have the victory. He died so that she might know that her child will live again. He died so that he might walk with her and talk with her when the pains of life tried to overwhelm her. He died so that, just as with the woman of Samaria, her ministry might be released and families dealing with AIDS all over the world might come to know the friendship of Jesus the Christ. He died so that she could become a bodacious woman. "Beams of heaven, as I go through this weary world below, guide my feet in peaceful ways, turn my midnights into days. For I do not know how long it will be or what the future holds for me, but this I know, if Jesus leads me, I shall get home someday!"[3]

Just Between Us

- What wells have you been drinking from?
- Have they been able to satisfy that inner thirst of your soul?
- What secret are you in need of sharing with someone for relief and support?
- What's making it "hot" in your life today?
- Living water will renew, refresh, and revive. Have you had a drink lately?
- From what places do you need to withdraw your investment of time and energy?
- Who are the folks you allow to star in your video?
- Are they truly stars?
- Have you had a divine "date" recently?

Suggestions

Find a secluded, quiet retreat center or Catholic monastery sitting far off the beaten path. Take a six-hour break, and go claim a space for you to sit and soak in the pleasure of a "divine date." Take some fruit and sparkling water, a wonderful stemmed glass, a cloth napkin, and a china plate, and spend some time with one of God's most awesome creations—you! Sit. Relax. Reflect. Listen to the quiet of your own spirit. Sit. Relax. Reflect. Write yourself a love letter to be read in three months.

chapter eight

≈

MS. PANDORA AND HER BOX
A STORY FOR MY YOUNGER SISTERS

Genesis 1:26–31

Once upon a time, in the place of legends and heroes, one of the ruling figures became angry at the men and their antics in the land. The men had discovered fire and its many uses, and for a while they seemed to feel that they too were mighty rulers. So the ruling god, Thor, decided to send the men upon the earth a gift to teach them a lesson. He created a beautiful woman. She had a dangerous, long weave and sculptured nails. Girlfriend was a brick house, really mighty, and letting it all hang out. Little sister was finely proportioned, beautiful of face, and truly had it going on! She descended from above with only the bare essentials on her back and a little box in her arms.

Thor had given her instructions before sending her to the earth. He told her not ever to open her box. He warned her that terrible tragedy would fall upon her and all of earth's inhabitants if the lid of the box was ever raised. Thor told her that she would get married and that the box she carried belonged to her husband. With that said, Thor sent Sister-girl on her way.

The men upon the earth were busy doing men things: hunting, fishing, golfing, and playing basketball and football. They kept busy fixing and repairing and seeking new things to conquer and destroy. Male bonding was in order. Male companionship was the word of the day. Brothers helped each other and stood by each other, for the world was theirs and theirs alone. But one day they looked up and saw a foreign object descending from the sky. They could not name it. They could not describe it. They could not figure out what it was. The boys in the hood were staring off into space, breathless, waiting to exhale. As Ms. Thang made her solo arrival, looking like pure brown sugar, she sweetly inquired, "Why are all eyes on me?"

As the men stood still, not knowing how to score, one of them, young, rich, and dangerous, pushed to the front, and shook his head free of his daydream to let the sister know that she had just entered a gansta's paradise. He stepped up to her, introduced himself as Mr. Smith, and declared to her, "Baby, we got it!" Since she was solo, totally fine, and unfamiliar with a man's need to score, she accepted his arm by faith, thinking she was off the hook. He took her to his house, where he sat her down and wondered what he was to do with both this creature and her little box.

Finally, he decided that he had better go and talk to his older brother, who lived a day's ride away. He told Ms. Thang to keep the doors locked and to stay busy and quiet until his return. For a while she busied herself looking and discovering. She touched things and looked under things. By nature she knew that the house could stand some order, so she began to clean. But even cleaning comes to an end.

As Mr. Smith arrived at his big brother's home and tried to explain the new creature who was at his home, he became worried and restless. Since his brother had never witnessed a woman, he had no advice, except for his little brother to keep her out of sight and to keep the lid fastened on her box. Mr. Smith left for home, dreaming about a new life with Ms. Thang. Meanwhile, back at the crib, Girlfriend had gotten bored. Being by herself was not pleasant, and she decided that she would not be treated like dog food, so, with an increasing faith in her sense of womanhood, she went and got her box. She looked at it. She stroked it. She wondered about it. She lifted it up. She put it down. She watched it. She touched the lid, which was shut tight. She walked to the window, but she did not see Mr. Smith. She waited for a few minutes and picked up the box again. She began to replay the instructions that Thor had given to her. What did he mean that the box belonged to her husband? Wasn't it her box? Wasn't it in her possession? Didn't she have any rights as a woman? Who was Thor to give her instructions anyway? He was off somewhere else, and she was here in a foreign place, all by herself. With those questions answered and her decision firmly made, she walked over to the table, picked up the box, and snatched open the lid. She became a bodacious woman.

All sorts of things flew up and around and out the door. With the blink of an eye, her box was empty, but she knew that something had changed. She slammed the lid back on her box, but it was too late. For as Mr. Smith made his approach to the house, he noticed weeds sprouting and storm clouds gathering; he saw disturbances and quarrels, even a group of men fighting, wrestling, and breaking the peace they had known before. He hurried to the house, and Ms. Thang met him at the door. But before he could enter, he was surrounded by other brothers who were trying to get in before him. That day Mr. Smith understood that there was a thin line between love and hate. And that was the beginning of all men trying to get Ms. Thang and to put their claim on her personal box.

What sort of deductions and summaries can we make from my twists on the classic story of Pandora's box? I have come to several conclusions:

1. The box that you have is definitely your own! Each one of us was sent to earth with our own personal box.
2. Some man somewhere is always going to try to take possession of your box. Little Sister, believe me, Mr. Smith is in the house!
3. There are those with higher authority who will try to put you in a box of limitations. Somebody will always want to tell you what you can and can't do with your box.
4. The media has decided that all black

women are on welfare, have no husbands, and are using their boxes to trap innocent men.

5. You also have a wisdom box, an intelligence box, and a mental box that you must decide what to do with. Regardless of what others think they know about you, only you have the real clue as to how wise and smart you are, and how much self-control you will have over your life.

6. You can make the wrong decisions and end up dead and in a box.

7. You can make some sound decisions that will allow you all control and power over that box you own.

Somebody wrote a song that says, "It's your thing, do what you want to do." But it's pretty obvious that this song was written before HIV and AIDS came on the scene. It's a funny incident in the story when Sister-girl tries to decide what to do with her box, but it's not about fun and games when *you* have to make this decision. Your selfhood, your personhood, and your self-esteem are in question. Choice, good decisions, and sound judgment are in question when you make a conscious decision to give some man your box. Yes, it is your thing, and you have the power to do what you want to do. But can you live with the consequences? Or are you ready to die from AIDS because of a stupid and uninformed decision?

The creator of Pandora put her in charge of her own box. He told her to give it only to her husband. That's the same lesson that the first woman, Eve, got when she was created by God. In our day, saving your box for a husband sounds as farfetched as riding a mule to school. Yet science has discovered that when you freely share your box with R. Kelly, Mr. Smith, Dog Food, and Q's Jook Joint, Baby Sister, you are allowing them to make deposits in your box that are guaranteed to pay dividends.

Some of us have been paid the dividend of having babies before we were ready. Having a baby is not a fatal dividend, but it is one that changes your life forever. Some of us have been paid the dividend of having to have abortions that have messed up our interiors and that will prevent us from becoming mothers when we feel we are ready. And some of those dead babies will haunt us for many years to come. Some of us have been paid the dividend of catching sexually transmitted diseases that might or might not be controlled by medicines prescribed by doctors. Too many of us have been paid the dividend of having the

HIV virus implanted into our warm and accepting centers, where it can lie dormant, waiting patiently for up to ten years before acting up, showing up, and being discovered.

My grandmother used to say that if you lie down with dogs, you will come up with fleas. Today, if you lie down with a dog, you're subject to come up with AIDS, for the commercials inform us that when you have sex with one person, you are actually having sex with all the other persons he has had sex with before you. Women are carriers too. If you pick up HIV, you pass it along to every man you have sex with, whether you know you have it or not. Oh yes, it is your thing, but, girlfriend, wise up and be discriminating about the use of your box. There is no cure for HIV or AIDS. A wooden box, a metal box, and a beautiful coffin are all the same. And that is the only future for someone with AIDS in the box!

Some man somewhere is always on the prowl. But you don't always have to be available. Just because a man wants does not necessarily mean he has to have. And, truly, he doesn't have to have yours. Men have some good lines, some convincing lines, and some sweet rap, but you need to use your head for more than a scarf holder. You need to make an honest decision about what's in this for you. If it's just a short-term thrill, is it worth it? If it's just about a date whenever he decides to come around, is it worth it? If it's about being popular and wanting to be with the "in" crowd, is it worth it? What is it that you want out of a relationship? What are your goals for friendship and commitment? What do you demand in return for sharing your unique self with another? What are the payoffs and dividends that you can realize? If you cannot come up with a positive score in your rating column, tell the brother goodbye! For many young men only want to cop and run. He ain't thinking about tomorrow, when you will be waiting by the phone for him to call. He ain't thinking about where diapers and formula are going to come from when the welfare check runs out before the month does. Baby sister, you had better think about what he's doing to you when he tries to talk his way into your box.

God did not die and leave anybody else in charge of your box. Pandora had to stop and think about her instructions from Thor. Remember, she asked herself, "Isn't this box mine? Isn't it in my possession? Don't I have rights as a woman?" And the answer to all of her questions was a loud, resounding *yes*. Don't ever allow anybody else to make decisions for you and your future. It is imperative that you have input into your future. No one else knows your dreams, your goals, and your aspirations. Your parents don't. The counselors don't. The pastor doesn't. Only God knows the future, and God gave you the ability to dream about your tomorrow. Never allow somebody else to put a lid on your hopes. Dream big dreams. See yourself doing the impossible. And go for the Olympic gold.

Because you are a woman, some folks have drawn boxes and put you in them. Racial-ethnic women ought to be teachers, nurses, and social workers, they say. That's a box. Racial-ethnic women don't need college; they ought to go to a vocational school and learn computer skills, they say. That's a box. Racial-ethnic women cannot achieve in business, succeed in politics, or thrive in math and science, they say. That's a box. You don't have to fit in their tiny boxes. Make your world larger. Allow your dreams to grow bigger. Daydream and see star-studded visions. Then plan your work and work your plan. Girlfriend, go for the gusto, and be all you can be! There is always tomorrow for the awarding of your prized box to another successful dreamer and achiever.

You have made a wise decision to get away

from the negative influences of the city's mean
streets. You have made a sensible judgment call
to remove yourself from the contrary effects of
ghetto life. You have used your common sense to
give yourself additional education, training, and
skills for life. You have to continue choosing every day what you want your life to become. It is
your video. You are the only person with the ability to become a shining star in the world that
you are creating. Don't let the wrong folks influence you. Don't allow some idiot to persuade you
to mess up, blow your game, and end up back
where you started. In your wisdom, intelligence,
and mental boxes, you have five senses, thinking
faculties, and the competence to know right from
wrong. Use what's in your box to make choices.
Don't permit some loser to take you down with
him.

Pandora opened her box and the whole world
turned upside down. When you don't stop and
think before opening up your box, your world
can get turned upside down too. Pandora didn't
have the opportunity to start over again. Troubles
began, confusion ran rampant, and that was the
end of her story. Thank God we have the golden
possibility of closing our box and starting all over
again. Have you had a baby? It's not the end of

your world. Have you left behind your lover? It's not the end of your world. Have you flunked out of public school? It's not the end of your world. Have you been too free with opening your box to R. Kelly, Mr. Smith, Dog Food, and Q's Jook Joint? It's not the end of your world. This is the moment of new beginnings. This is the instant of fresh starts. This is the time for a stimulating commencement. Decide now to close the lid on your box and to become a woman of discerning taste. Decide now to enlarge the world of your mental and emotional and intellectual box and to take charge of your life as never before. Decide now that you will not end up in a closed box before old age. Decide now what dividends you want from life, and set your sights on worthwhile goals. Hold on to your box. If the right man comes along, take your time; think long and hard. Always remember that Pandora's man didn't have a clue as to what to do with her, and most of the ones trying to take the lid off your box won't know either!

Just Between Us
- Is your name Pandora?
- Did you take the lid off your box too soon, not realizing the troubles coming your way?

- Have you fallen for any good lines recently?
- Do you know anyone who has died from AIDS?
- Do you know that babies can be born with AIDS?
- Do you understand that every day can be a new start for you?
- Have you learned the value of daydreaming, setting goals, and envisioning a better life?
- How much self-determination do you practice over your wisdom, intelligence, mental, and spiritual boxes?
- You were given a gift by the Creator of life. What do you plan to do with it?

Suggestions

Take a survey of three women who you know well and trust: find one who is in college or a recent college graduate; find a woman in her thirties who is not married and has no children but has a very good profession; and find a woman who is married and working, has children, and is in her forties. Tell these women the tale of Pandora, and ask them how the story has applied to their lives. Learn from the stories they share. Recognize that neither Pandora nor Eve started all the evil in the world. The satanic, which is older than either of them, began sinful practice by trying to compete with God in the heavens. This is not a woman-bashing story but a woman-helping one!

chapter nine

~

THE PRODIGAL DAUGHTER
EVERY WOMAN

Luke 15:11–32

Once upon a time, in a place far away, there was a man who came to seek and save those who were lost. This man ate with sinners, associated with women of the night, and loved little children. The leaders of his day were disturbed by the company he kept, for they had different standards and measuring rods for those who could be accepted and received. These leaders avoided anyone who might be suspect. They set up barriers to keep out those whom they judged inferior to them. And they challenged Jesus to do the same.

One day, Jesus took the time to try to explain God's generous love to these leaders. Jesus told them some stories to help them see just how valuable all people are to God. Jesus told them how

God is like a shepherd who leaves ninety-nine sheep to search for one sheep who has strayed away. They didn't get the message. He told them that God is like a woman who calls in her neighbors to help her search for one wedding coin that has been lost from her dowry. They still couldn't comprehend God's grace, love, and capacity for forgiveness.

Finally, Jesus said, "Let me try one more story. Let's talk about God being a parent. Let's talk about God having only two children. Let's see if you can comprehend how God's love for us is like that of a parent." Then Jesus told the story that has been called the Gospel of the Gospel. Jesus painted a word picture of God's love, which allows us the freedom of our actions. This love lets us test our limits, explore our space, and bump our heads. This love waits on us, watches for us, and rejoices over us when we return. I want to interpret this age-old story for women.

None of the women in the story have names. Like Alice Walker's characters, we have been rendered invisible, of little consequence, and not worthy to be called by a name because of the plight of black women in this society. But every woman is a certain woman. Every woman has the potential to become a bodacious woman. And the two daughters in the story represent each one of us.

History has always recorded the legends of matriarchal societies, where women had the power, the knowledge, and the right to rule. So it is not surprising that the mother in this story represents God. She stands in as the one who rules, the one who is in charge. She depicts our God, who has enormous wealth, and is generous with her love.

A certain bodacious woman has two daughters. The youngest of them says to her mother, "If you were to die, I'd be rich. If you were to die, the courts would award me so much of your property that I could go anywhere I wanted to go. I could do what I wanted to do, I could hang out with whoever I wanted. I'd rag down. I'd ride well. I'd get away from you and this little hick town. If you would just hurry up and die, I'd really be able to begin to live."

What Sister-girl is saying in essence is, "I wish you were dead!" How awful is the reality that a daughter could actually feel this way. But we understand that our little sister is young, single, and naive. She assumes that if she could only get her hands on enough money, that money would buy her freedom. She feels that money would expand her world and remove all of her limitations. With enough money, she could leave the authority of her mother. She could be shed of the control of her mother. She would be liberated from the rules and regulations of her mother. If she could just leave home, she would be footloose and fancy-free. Wild Thang would be her new name. She longs to have freedom and to be a liberated woman. She says to her mother, "Release me; let me go!" In her heart, she is already gone.

Many of us were once like this daughter. Many of us remember our dreams about lives that were contrary to community norms. Many of us remained in the physical confines of our parents' home, but in our hearts, we too had already gone to the far country.

Mother stands there and listens. This mother knows about the far country. This mother knows about the school of hard knocks, the college of rejection, and the university of isolation. And Mother knows best. So, with pain in her heart and tears in her eyes, she pleads with her daughter not to go there. Mother begs her child to stay at home and tells her that she does not need the difficult lessons of the far county. Mother does not want her baby to bump her head and bruise

her tail feathers. Mother knows. But Sister-girl is
determined and haughty. She will not repent. She
will not change her mind. So Mother sells a few
apartment buildings to liquidate some fluid cash.
She takes a dozen furs to Fairy Godmother's Place
for resale. She calls the local Infiniti and Lexus
dealers and sells her fleet of specially designed
stretch limos. She gets the stockbroker to liquidate a third of her investment portfolio. She gives
little sister some Diana Ross-sized diamond ear-
rings and some Patti LaBelle-sized diamond rings
to keep as insurance. She allows little sister to go
through her closet and fill the Louis Vitton and
Fendi luggage with every designer name for her
trip into the far country. Then, with an achy-
breaky heart, Mother watches her step into her
private jet for the journey into the far country.

It's a sad story but very real. For it is part of
the cycle of life that daughters must leave Mother's
house. Part of the drama of our existence is the
truth that a daughter will grow to hate her mother
in order to leave her and home. Every daughter
wrestles with how she will leave. Every daughter
struggles with where she will go. Every daughter
grapples with how will she make it on her own.
Oh yes, the longing for the far country comes
into the heart of every daughter. We can all iden-

tify with Sister-girl who has finally made the break and goes into the far country.

We do not know whether the far country is very far away in this story. The parable of parables allows us to use our imagination, because in every age the far country is a different place. For women my age, the South Side of Chicago used to be the far country. Detroit, with men who worked in the big money-making auto plants, was a far country. New York's Harlem and the valleys of California used to be our far country. The name of the city and its location do not make any difference. Whenever we want to run away and forget Mama and Mama's God, Girlfriend, we are in the far country. Wide is the road. Attractive are the lights. But the far country is the direct way to hell and destruction. The road leads downward all the way, for the highway is built on a downgrade. There is no need to trudge, sweat, or toil. You can just slip and slide, bump and grind, butterfly and line dance until you bang up against the gates of your limitations, which is hell.

Needless to say, Sister-girl arrives in the far country in grand style, dressed, pressed, and ready to mess over anybody who wants to slow her row. She has a fine condo, live-in help, unlimited food and liquor. Drugs? No problem. Just say the word. Lonely? Never. People, people everywhere, and just look at the assortment of men!

With live DJs blasting boom boxes and hot CDs, every day is a party: singing, dancing, laughing, spending, having a ball; doing it to death with tall men, short men, young men and old, men with money, men with none, men with ambitions, men with schemes, men with plans, and men planning games; always a crowd, always plenty of liberties. Sister just parties till she drops. The crowd is maddening, the faces blend together, drinking, drugs, having parties and sex. There are no rules. There are no values. There is no one to stop the fun. If it feels good, just do it. If anything runs out, just buy more. Welcome to the far country.

But time simply waits, and time will tell. "What do you mean, there is no more? There must be a mistake. They can't put me out of here. I own the place." Well, she knows that her friends will cover her for a minute. She can just hang with them.

Nina Simone said it best: *"Nobody wants you when you are down and out."* [1] And Sister didn't even have an AT&T calling card to call home!

But the road to hell does not stop when the

money runs out. Sister-girl keeps slipping down the road, and there does not seem to be a return road up: flophouses and cheap hotel rooms; turning tricks for meals; sleeping with dogs and coming up with fleas, crabs, and AIDS. She can't look in the mirror, tries to block out the pain, the too smooth liquor, the too tough drugs, and the too many abortions, tries to cover the too many acts of illicit and unsafe sex.

Homeless, without a change of clothes, Girlfriend ends up in the far country's suburbs, working as a live-in maid. One day she is down on her knees, scrubbing the lady's floor, with a head rag hiding a head that ain't seen a beauty shop; the curl and the weave are both gone. Her fingernails cannot even remember acrylic, and her feet look as if pedicures do not exist. A bright idea comes to Sister-girl's mind: "I think I'll get up and go back home." The parable says that the child comes to herself. The Greek term that Luke uses describes an individual who has just awakened from a fainting spell.

When you are unconscious, you are not aware of your actions. When you are unconscious, you are not responsible for your activities and movements. When you are unconscious, you are not cognizant of people, places, or things. When you are unconscious, you are not accountable for what you say. But one day, you wake up. One day, you return to your right mind. One day, you are fully aware of who you are, where you are, and how you got there. One day, you wake up and remember whose you are. Thank God, one day you become fully awake to see yourself as you really are.

When Sister-girl comes to herself, she recognizes her sin. She does not try to shirk her responsibility but acknowledges the wrong she has done: "I have sinned against the God of heaven. And I have sinned against my mother." Unlike most of us, she is able to admit that her sin has affected others. When she comes to herself, she says, "I think I'll get up and go home. Mama has housekeepers, maids, and cooks. Each one of them has plenty to eat and a room with a television and a phone. Surely, Mama will hire me as a housekeeper." And the curtain comes down on the end of the scene, as the drama shifts to a waiting, loving mother who is a bodacious woman.

Now, keep in mind that with this parable, Jesus is trying to teach the church leaders about the reckless love of God. So he images God as a mother who goes out each day and searches the horizon, watching for her child to come home. Mother knew that unchecked spending and undisciplined living would break her daughter down. Mother knew that hard knocks would get her attention. Mother knew that the pain of rejection would soon send her home. So this mother waits and daily watches for her daughter to return from the far country.

The drama moves us to the reunion of mother and daughter. We see a repentant daughter who asks forgiveness and a loving mother who grants it. The scripture describes embracing and continual kissing. The kiss was a sign of reconciliation. The kiss meant that forgiveness was granted. The kiss meant that the hurt of yesterday had been healed.

The best designer dress is ordered. This mother gives the message to all who are standing around that her child is welcome in her home. A huge, staggering, multicarat diamond is put on Sister's finger. It is the symbol of authority granted to every member of this family. Mother is saying with the ring, "All that I have belongs to my child." Then Mother says, "Call Farrangomo's and order some of his best kidskin leather shoes. Nothing but the best for my child who was lost. No Payless, no Naturalizers, not even Joseph Weitzmans will do. I want the best for her feet."

Then, Mother calls the cook and says, "We

are having a party for the whole community. Tell the staff to send invitations to everyone so we can welcome my child back home. All of y'all come too. For the daughter who went to sleep, this girl who had a mental lapse, has come to herself and come home. I invite all of you who called me a fool when I gave her my money. I invite all of you who talked about me as you saw me watch for her day by day. I invite all of you who made bets that she'd never amount to anything. And I surely invite all of you who sat with me at my kitchen table and cried with me and held my hands as you remembered when your daughter acted the very same way. I want all of you to come on. We're having a party. My daughter is home! She has become a bodacious woman, and I want the world to know it!"

Wouldn't it be wonderful if this third scene of an awesome homecoming celebration was the end of the story? Wouldn't it be a good ending to a horrible story? This is such a neat and happy conclusion. Wouldn't it be nice to stop right here, close the book, and say, "the end"? But there is an even sadder tale to be told. For we are a variety of women; one size and one story do not fit us all. And Jesus gave us this story about every woman.

For the mother has an older daughter. She is the sister who stayed home. She is the good daughter who never disobeyed, never got out of line, and never left Mama's house. Can't you just hear her, standing outside the party? "Here I am, the good daughter. Why can't Mother notice me? Here I am, acting like her servant, doing all the work, and she's making a big to-do over my sister! Mother has never given me a party. She gave that heifer money to waste. She allowed her to go off and have a good time. I never got a diamond ring. That cow has had every man in town. And Mama is in there acting like she's so holy. How can Mama be so stupid? Surely Mama can't forget that she has shacked up, had abortions, and done drugs. But I've had to sneak for every minute of fun I've ever had. Mama never even knew about my abortions. I kept my reputation clean. I hate both of them."

Girlfriend cannot celebrate. This oldest daughter has remained home, has faithfully obeyed, but has resented every task assigned. She has followed orders, but with no joy in her heart. She has gone to church, but she never found God. She has served on committees, has held offices, has worked in the kitchen, and has chaired various working groups, but she is not a happy camper.

She has pasted a phony smile on her face, but it doesn't come from within her heart. Now her lips are stuck out, her jaws are tight, and her nose is flared. No way will she pretend she is happy to see the daughter who dared to escape!

Do you know her feelings? Can you identify with her pain? If you have always been the "good daughter," if you've never gone to the far country, if you've never been bold enough to test your limitations openly, don't you feel superior? For this story is equally about the daughter who left the house, did her thing, and came back to ask forgiveness, and about the daughter who stayed home and was lost in the house. For we like to think that God has more love for those of us who stay in the church building. We like to feel that we have seniority and special favor with God. But this God, who loves us like a generous mother, loves both daughters just the same. This is amazing grace.

God's love for each one of us is so great that we are sought for and rejoiced over when we return. Even when we have gone our own way, done our own thing, been to hell, and enjoyed the stay—if we want to, we can come home. We can be rebellious, immature, foolish, and wasteful of the teachings and love that have been bestowed upon us. But love is willing us to come home. Love wants to forgive us. Love wants to love us into being our best.

Love says that there are no superior or inferior daughters in the family. Love says that resentment has no place and that all of us are welcome at the table. Love says that reconciliation can be ours. We are yet sisters, daughters, whether we left or stayed. Each one of us is a daughter. Which daughter are you?

I know that I was the younger daughter. I left home and went straight to the far country. I did everything and everybody I could, and enjoyed doing it. Oh yes, I went there and I did that. And just like the story goes, I hit bottom. I found myself with men who had nothing, and with nothings who tried to pass themselves off as men. I tried sex that wasn't free or safe and stayed out there so long that I almost wiped out thoughts of Mama's God. But one day, I found that I couldn't go any lower. I was in the pits, scratching on the bottom. On that day, I came to myself. That was the day I regained consciousness. On that day, I remembered what I had left at home. Jesus welcomed me home. He had been waiting all the time.

It really makes no difference which daughter

you are. For today, you simply need to accept that you are a sinner in need of God's amazing grace. You need to realize that God wants you to be at home, in the house of love. You can accept God's forgiveness for your attitude of rebellion or your attitude of resentment. You can accept your sister as a daughter of love. You can reach out to her and welcome her into the family of love. Today, we can celebrate that all of us have a family and we have a home. Love waits for you and for me. Come home! Come home! You who are weary, come on home! Be that bodacious woman today!

Just Between Us

- Do you feel stuck at home being the "good daughter"?
- Have you discovered that you really can be lost in Mama's house?
- Are you trying to get to the far country?
- Have you been in the far country?
- How did you leave Mama's?
- In your unconscious state, what things did you do that now require your amends?
- Have you discovered that you really can go home?

- Have you ever had a welcome party thrown in your honor?
- Can you imagine God as a loving, waiting, forgiving mother?
- Whose feelings most closely match yours, the little sister or the good daughter?
- Does it really make any difference?

Suggestions

Plan a welcome celebration for the newest women in your local church or work situation. Have every sister bring a small token to remind the new women that they are loved.

Do something special to recognize young sisters in your congregation who are just entering their teens. Let them know you have great expectations of their lives.

Organize a "thank you" time for the senior women who have held down the fort and made sacred space available for you.

~

chapter ten

Too Legit to Quit

2 Samuel 21:1–14

Like many of you, I have had the pleasure of having two living grandmothers. My mother was birthed by one sister, Lucinda, in Mississippi. But she was raised, from the age of eight, by the other sister, Eunice, in Gary, Indiana. In their later years, the two sisters lived together in Gary and took care of us and each other. It was always understood and assumed that both of my grandmothers would die before my mother. That's usual. So, when my Big Mama, Eunice, began to exhibit behavior that looked like Alzheimer's disease, I tried to prepare her sister, my mother, and myself for her eventual death. Little did I know what would happen next.

On May 18, 1986, my fifty-nine-year-old mother, Doretha, had a major stroke and was in a coma for twelve days. My seven siblings and I gathered and stayed with her around the clock.

On the eleventh day, the neurosurgeon told us
that Mama's brain wave activities were diminishing and that we had to decide whether to continue to hold her on life support or to terminate
it and let her go home to be with God. I need
not try to describe the pain, agony, and debate of
siblings. I need not spend time talking about our
grief and utter confusion over a decision of this
proportion. But I do want to share with you the
fact that when the decision to terminate life support was made, there was another big matter to
determine. Should the grandmothers be told now
or later?

My mother's birth mother, Lucinda, was
eighty-three, and her other mother, Eunice, was
eighty. They both walked with the aid of canes.
Their hearing was diminished. Their recent
memory had begun to fade and their voices were
getting feeble. But we decided that collectively
they were responsible for Doretha's life, and if
she was going to die, they had to make the choice
to be with her or not. It became my duty, as the
oldest grandchild, to be the bearer of news to
them.

I will never forget that long ride of six blocks
from the hospital to their home. It was a lovely

spring day, May 30, and both of them were sitting outside on the screened porch. They seemed to be waiting for something. When I got out of the car, both of them stood at the same time. I replayed all of the decisions that had been made and asked if they wanted to return to the hospital with me or to wait until Mom died.

My Big Mama, the one with Alzheimer's, looked me in the eye and said, "We've been with that gal all of her life, and we'll be with her until the end." There was no further discussion. There was no argument or debate. Both of these old and stately women returned with me to that hospital room. We gathered around my mother's bed. We sang to her, we each talked to her, and we prayed for her. We each gave her permission to cease the struggling and to go on home to be with God.

I couldn't stand there and watch the slowly fading monitors. I left the room and went into the hallway. But those two stalwart, bodacious women that were my grandmothers never left my mother's side. And when she breathed her life into eternity, they were there. She was their child, and she was too legit for them to ever quit.

I don't know the anguish of a mother who has to watch a part of herself die. I don't know the grief of women like my grandmothers or like Mary, the mother of Jesus, or like Rizpah in the Hebrew Scriptures. But these bodacious women, in their sufferings, stand for millions of us. Silently and often alone, they teach us how to bear sorrow with grace, dignity, and perseverance. For the ones we bring into the world are precious, and we refuse to give up on them. It makes no difference whether they are dope dealers, drug users, prostitutes, whores, abusers, or the misused—we keep holding on to them. We won't give up on them. And seldom do we leave them all alone.

As far as I'm concerned, Sister Rizpah suffered greater tribulation than any other woman in the Hebrew Scriptures. For five months, from the fall barley harvest until the early spring rains, she watched over the seven dead, decaying bodies of her two sons and King Saul's five grandsons. The name Rizpah has come to mean intense suffering. This sister is a woman who stood strong for her community, endured personal and painful struggle, and held out until liberation came from God. She was only one of Saul's wives and concubines. The five grandsons had mothers and grandmothers, but the text does not give us the reasons for these women's absence. What we find is a bodacious woman, Rizpah, refusing to forsake these who had been accursed and killed, high on a hill, for sins that Saul had committed before his death.

A three-year famine had made King David ask God for a reason. He learned that the sin of Saul had brought death into the land. The tribe that had been wronged wanted absolution in the form of the death of all of the sons of Saul. King David spared only the crippled son of his best friend, Jonathan. The other boys were killed. I'm positive that all of the mothers wept and wailed. I know internally that each mother pleaded, prayed, and petitioned God for the lives of their innocent sons. But they were not able to stop the seizure and murder of these seven young men. Most likely these grieving women had withdrawn into their mourning and were surrounded by friends and family. It was Rizpah who determined that she would stand watch over the seven dead, decaying bodies so that no further dishonor would be done to them. As far as she was concerned, not just her two sons but all seven of the boys were too legit for her to quit!

Taking a sackcloth, Rizpah spread it out to shield herself by day and to rest on by night. Stifled by the heat of day, chilled by the cold of night, Rizpah remained near those sun-scorched, weird-looking, air-blackened, dishonored, and decaying bodies. She watched and guarded to ensure them no further harm. Sometimes standing, sometimes sitting, sometimes drugged from the lack of a decent meal and sleep, with brave effort and absolute determination, she drove away the dogs, waved away the vultures, and kept back the scavengers and predators that wanted to take the very last of her sons.

Verse 9 says the boys were "exposed . . . on the mountain before the Lord." This was not done in some private, solitary valley. Their bodies were displayed in public where they and she were exposed to the whole wide world. Alone on a weary rock, day after day, week after week, month after month, for five long months, Rizpah stayed there with those seven dead, decaying bodies. Passersby gazed from a distance. Some folks pitied her. Some folks mocked her. Some folks made fun of her and the strange company she chose to keep. Some folks called her mad. Some most likely talked about her great courage. But all of them did their talking from a distance.

There was no support group. There was no kitchen committee. There was no networking chain from which to draw strength. This sister, like too many of us, had to stand all alone. But she was bodacious and too legit to quit.

It had been only a couple of years since Saul had died. Rizpah was without a man. When he had died, she lost her place in the royal palace and the queenly clothes that went with her position. When Saul had died, she had been claimed by his general, who was slain shortly thereafter in battle. And now she had lost her two sons. There was no welfare. There were no government subsidies. There were no federal grants for displaced homemakers. So, Girlfriend made a tent out of sackcloth, spread it on a rock, and made herself a committee of one for the safekeeping of seven dead, decaying, stinking bodies.

An artist by the name of Turner painted a picture of Rizpah. He tries to help us visualize the extreme suffering of this, our sister. The picture shows the seven bodies lying on a rock, covered with sackcloth. Rizpah has her face covered with one hand; with the other she waves a lighted torch to frighten off wild animals. A lion crouches nearby, and a vulture or buzzard circles overhead. But the picture does not do justice to the Rizpahs I have seen and watched in my lifetime.

I have seen bodacious black women keep "scavengers" away. I know bodacious black women who have stood alone to accomplish great feats for the community. This woman in scripture exemplifies what many of us endure over and over again. I am persuaded that the seven dead, decaying, stinking bodies stand for something essential to each one of us. I am fully persuaded that the God we serve placed Rizpah in our midst for such a time as this.

We know today that the number seven stands for the completion of a cycle. It means we have come full circle. It means it's time for an old ending and a new beginning. So it was to teach us a lesson about how to become bodacious women that this sister stood there. She simply stood her ground. She didn't try to steal the bodies and run away. She stood there. She didn't give up, get discouraged, and simply fade away. She stood there in our place to represent how we guard, watch, and care for our homes, our communities, and the black church.

Rizpah stood there to show us how to stand firm in the face of struggle and terrific pain and grief. I believe that those seven dead, stinking bodies portray items in our life today. These are the things we stand and fight for, day after day, week after week, month after month. These are the things for which we give up our comforts and deny ourselves many of the pleasures that life affords. These are the things we hold near and dear to our hearts.

For me, these seven dead, stinking bodies are symbols. The first body represents our black men. The decimation of black males affects and touches each one of us. We birth them. We raise them. We love them. And, we know them for who they really are as they get caught up, swept away, and mowed down right before our eyes. The majority of us will not diss them and walk off seeking men of other races. We stand by our black men.

The second body symbolizes our black children. Drugs, gangs, teen pregnancies, and school push-outs and dropouts make our hearts heavy as we watch our children throw away their lives. We don't give up on them, but we will stand up for them, snatch a knot in them, and still stand with them all the way. Even though drugs have entered our lives and have affected too many of our children, we stand with them.

The third body symbolizes the black church. The black church still abuses women. The black church yet tries to push us aside and to hold us down and back. The black church yet uses women. It wants and needs our attendance, our money, and our services, but it doesn't allow women to share power. Yet we continue to stand for the black church. Without our planning, giving, supporting, and attending, there would be no black church, or any other church for that matter! Cry, yell, and scream we will, as we stand with the black church.

Body number four is the black male power brokers in both the church and the community. We have fought, bled, and died to keep Anglos from treating us the way we allow black men to treat us. But we don't give up. We won't quit. We have never washed our hands of them. We stand alongside them in spite of themselves.

Our hard-earned positions in society and the church are the fifth body. Glass ceilings, stained glass ceilings, sexual harassment, token raises, and meaningless titles try to discourage us and to make us accept less than we are due. But in the struggle for equality in both the world and the church, we are committed to stand firm and not to turn our backs and walk away. We do what needs to be done. We do without credit and often without recognition. We stand.

The black race, our nation, our people is the sixth dead, stinking body. For black folks seem to be running backward. We keep forgetting our history and repeating the past. It seems as if we refuse to wake up and band together for more than survival. Yet bodacious black women keep waving sackcloth. We keep shouting out warnings. We get tired and want to give up. People call us fools for crying out about equal rights, inclusion, and equality. But we won't give up. We stand faithfully on the Word of God that "whosoever the Son sets free, is free indeed!" (John 8:36). God said it. We believe it. We stand on it!

The last body, which is exposed, swinging, and most quickly decaying, depicts the way we treat ourselves. We tend always to put ourselves last. We have become workaholics, careaholics, foodaholics, and perfectionists who take on the guilt of the whole world and hate ourselves in the process. But, Sister-girl, our day has come! Our time under God is now! The reign of freedom has been announced. We can leave the hill and return to living fully!

Rizpah stood from the beginning of the barley season until the rains came. It was then that King David sent men to take down the bones, retrieve the hidden bodies of Saul and Jonathan, and give all of them a decent burial. All of this was possible because of Rizpah and her standing, which had not been in vain. And, Sister-girl, neither has ours!

Can you just imagine Rizpah standing there, watching for a cloud? Can you even begin to conceive her joy as she saw the darkening of the skies? Can you picture her anticipation when she felt the moisture forming in the air? For when the rains came, it meant that her days of sackcloth wearing were over. When the rains came, it meant that her holding on to threads, waving rags, and being vigilant, alone, while others watched and recorded her story had come to a screeching halt! David had noticed what she had done. The king had honored her steadfastness. The king had valued her commitment. And, most important, God had vindicated the boys! God honored her stand. God recognized her labor. And God had her history recorded so that centuries later, other mothers could stand and be bodacious women for their sons.

It was on a day we have labeled Good Friday that on a hill called Calvary, the Child of God and of Mary was crucified for a sin he had not committed. John's Gospel says, "Standing at the foot of the cross was his mother, Mary." The hands that had created the universe were fastened to the cross. The one who had commanded the wind and mastered the sea was stretched out as a spectacle of misery and shame. The one who had thrown the stars into orbit and set the sun blazing in the sky was hung between heaven and earth, high on a hill, dying for you and for me. And standing there were bodacious women.

The government had condemned Mary's son. Mary refused to hide in shame. His crucifixion was the ultimate symbol of public rejection and humiliation. Mary would not forsake him. His heart was broken. His character had been defamed. His integrity had been impugned. His reputation had been smeared. His good name was ruined. Yet Mary stood with him at the foot of the cross.

When the disciples had run out on him, when those he had fed and raised from the dead refused to come to his side, his mother was there. She did not crouch down in shame. She did not faint or stumble. Like Rizpah, she just stood there. Surrounded by a cruel, vicious, and angry mob thirsty for blood, she would not be moved. She couldn't kiss his hands and make them better. She couldn't wipe his brow and make the pain go away. She couldn't even stop the soldier from piercing his tender side. But what she could do was stand there while her baby boy was dying. While her son was being killed and her heart was breaking, she felt that he was too legit for her to quit. So she stood there. She had agreed to bring him into the world, and she was determined to stand with him as he breathed his life away. The record shows that, bold, beautiful, and bodacious, his mother was there.

Just as with Lucinda, Eunice, Rizpah, and Mary, God honors our faithfulness. God honors our stand. God honors our determination to hang in there during the rough and stormy times of life. When the devil thought that "the end" was written, the Resurrection brought the rains. Rain means refreshment. Rain means new life. Rain means a new beginning. Rain means it's starting-over time. Regardless of what you have been standing and waiting for, look up and see the rain on the horizon, for rain is on its way toward you.

You can make it if you simply determine that you will continue to stand. Regardless of who refuses to go along with you, stand. Those seven dead, decaying, and stinking bodies can have new life. Remember that God asked Elijah, "Can these bones live?" (Ezekiel 37:3) and bleached bones came together with the breath of new life. Bodacious woman, dead bones are not the end!

I personally know about those seven dead, decaying, and stinking bodies. I personally know about standing high upon a hill and having even family members think I was a fool. My first dead body was a father who raped me repeatedly. The second was a mother who repeatedly refused to see my pain. The third body was my former husband, who was as abusive as "dear old Dad." Fourth was my belonging to a denomination that said, "You don't belong. You are not charismatic enough." Fifth was a denomination that said, "You don't belong. You are too charismatic." Sixth was my own biological children: a beloved older son who got tangled up with the law while an officer; a middle son who is a college grad and often behaves like he's uneducated; and an only daughter who came home from college not with a degree but with my grandson!

These incidents made me want to give up. These situations made me want to quit, run away, and hide. These events made me want to sit down and refuse ever to stand again. And then there was the seventh dead, stinking, decaying body, which was intense dislike of myself. I was critical of me and everybody else. I didn't like me or anybody else. I was so afraid that people would see my past, my pain, my hurt and scars, and accuse me of inflicting my own wounds. So I kept away from people and didn't even want to know myself. But, thank God, one day the rains blew into my life. One day, in a clinical pastoral education class, God sent the rain of tears, which broke the dam and allowed the sun to peek inside my dry and thirsty soul. That day, God showed me how my stand had been honored. That day was the initial visualization of my becoming a bodacious woman!

The Holy Spirit brought release and healing into my soul. The fresh winds of the Holy Spirit swept away the old fears and left power, love, and a transformed mind in their place. And today I declare unto you that I'm standing on the promises and not just surviving on the premises. My name was Rizpah, for I do know great suffering. But one day, I told Jesus it would be all right if he changed my name. Talk about a child who does love Jesus—here is one! And he's too legit for me to quit!

Just Between Us

- Have you been standing alone for a long time?
- Have you really felt that no one else knows your pain?
- Can you believe that God has been with you and for you all the time?
- Recognize that "standing" for this issue may

be over soon, but there will always be hills to stand upon. Are you ready to come down off the hill?

- What "decaying and stinking body" in your life is worst right now and needs work?
- What signs of coming rain have you experienced?

Suggestions

Commit to spend time in a battered women's shelter or a home for pregnant teens.

Begin to teach your sons and grandsons how to be responsible and to value you and other women.

Allow the significant men in your life to "be men." Stop trying to fix all situations.

Join forces with other women who are working on their "dead, stinking bodies." Support groups of every type are available in your area.

Begin to use inclusive language. Begin to talk about the need for inclusive language with others.

Read materials and start a study group around the issue of women being passed over and left out in the formation of history.

Volunteer to serve on committees where

women are few, at work, in your city, and in your church. Make yourself available, and take a stand.

Commit to taking better care of yourself!

If the glass or stained glass ceiling has bumped your head too many times, ask God for the wisdom to start your own business and to find a place without limits.

chapter eleven

≈

It Takes a Thief
The Story of Queen Esther

Book of Esther

Chuck and I were walking through the airport when a newspaper headline caught my eye. It took up almost one-half of the front page and screamed, "They Robbed You!" Being the curious woman that I am, I stopped to see who "they" were and to better understand what they had taken from me. For if something belongs to me, I want it. If I have earned it, especially the old-fashioned way, I feel I deserve it. I don't want anybody to take something that is rightfully mine.

People who know me will testify that I am a generous woman. I love to share my resources. I enjoy giving money and things to those in my life. I have a wealthy spirit, for I have come to realize that the more I give, the more I can receive. But please know that I don't want you to try to take anything away from me. I desire to extend myself, but I don't want to be robbed.

I read the newspaper further. It wanted me to believe that the baseball players and owners had robbed me by their selfish decision not to play. I decided not to waste my anger energy on this particular robbery. I don't like or watch baseball, so I was not personally involved. But I know there is always the other side of the story.

One Sunday, a woman in my local congregation was going to her garage to get into her car, to take her own money and buy herself some new tires. As she entered her garage, a thief snatched her purse and ran to a getaway car. Can you imagine her feelings at that moment? Can you begin to comprehend that it takes a real thief to decide that what she owned the thief had a right to take? This individual had to have plotted, planned, and schemed how to take something that day without asking. This thief had no regard for violating this sister's space. It was her garage. The thief hurt her feelings. Her credit cards and her checkbook were now out of her control. The thief made her and each of us feel vulnerable and unsafe, for you never know when the thief will show up at *your* garage.

Sometimes it takes a thief to help us understand that things are not of ultimate importance. Our sister was not hurt or left in the garage dead, so the thief allowed her to experience the goodness of God, the protection of God, and the provisions of God. On that occasion, she discovered that she was a true bodacious woman. She gave up what she had, and God had her purse returned later that day with only the cash missing. What the thief meant for evil, God turned around. Her situation reminded me of Queen Esther's.

The book of Esther, which never mentions the name of God, details how a nation was saved and delivered from the hands of a powerful man in the kingdom who was only a thief. Haman, a high government official with the authority of the king, had decided that what did not belong to him—that is, the lives and property of innocent, displaced Jews—he had a right to exterminate. Haman plotted, planned, and determined to wipe out the entire population of Jews. Talk about ethnic cleansing! He had no regard for their posterity. He didn't care that they were vulnerable. He knew they were unprotected, as they didn't own any land and had no political clout. They didn't have economic power, so he thought they were without help or resources. His intent

was to kill them all, to wipe them and their existence from the face of the earth. And his hatred
for a nation was based on his personal animosity
toward one Jewish man.

This is a familiar scene that was repeated by
Stalin and Hitler against more recent generations
of Jews. And let us not forget that this same plot
was perpetuated against black people by those
who were determined that we were to be the per-
petual slaves of Anglos because they had determined we were inferior. We were stolen from our
own land and brought to this place where we
could own no land. We had no political power,
for we were not allowed to vote. We had no economic power, for we were to work only to ad-
vance Anglos' security. We looked like we had no
assistance or help. They planned to prevent us
from getting an education so that our ignorance
would slowly eradicate us. When slavery didn't
kill us and we were emancipated, they plotted
against us by deliberately infecting African men
with syphilis, which they refused to treat. When
this plot wasn't effective enough, they moved to
distribute drugs in our communities so that we
would kill ourselves. This plot seems to be the
best one they have come up with yet.

But when Haman went to work on his plan

and it was revealed to that bodacious woman
Queen Esther, she went and declared to the king,
"We have a foe and a wicked enemy who has plotted for us to be destroyed, killed, and annihilated"
(7:3–4). Bodacious women in our time need to
wake up and understand that we have similar foes.
It is no coincidence that dope, violence, and murder are on a rampage in our communities. There
is a thief who wants to wipe us out. Jesus declares
in John 10:10, "The thief comes only to steal
and kill and destroy; I have come that they may
have life, and have it abundantly."

Because of the praying and planning that
Esther and Mordecai and the sisters in Esther's
network did, the Jews were saved. Esther had to
go through the process of realizing who she was,
where she was, and why she was in that place at
that time. When the lightbulb came on, she declared, "If I perish, I perish. I'm going to see the
king!" (4:16). Her personal welfare was placed
on the back burner as the saving of an entire nation came into play.

Our community needs us. Our community is
depending on us. And so is God. It's our time to
be bodacious women. It's our time to act like
bodacious women. It's our time to get involved
in the way bodacious women always have. The

doors of our churches have always remained open due to the love, work, and sacrifice of bodacious women. Newspapers have been started, schools have been established, and self-help organizations and penny savings banks have been chartered by bodacious women. Because of our love for God and our concern for our people, we have been willing to put our personal safety and welfare aside, prop open the doors of the church, and say to the community, "Here is a safe place, here is a refuge, here is a place that all of us own and can use for our advancement."

The story of Esther is not a very pretty one when we get to the end of it. Mordecai, her kinsman, pimped Esther! She had been an orphan left in his care. He realized her beauty and decided to put her in the "beauty contest" for queen. His advice to her was, "Smile, keep your mouth shut, and pass as one of them." Esther did not tell folks that she was a Jew. She followed Mordecai's advice and became just another pretty face. She won the contest. She was selected and then trained for a year in how to please her man. Her mind was not important. Her intelligence was not the thing. Her education and knowledge were not uplifted. But she was taught how to make a man sexually happy and satisfied. She was trained for a year in how to be a "thing." This was the destiny that her male relative felt was appropriate for her. She went along with the scheme.

Mordecai gloried in her spunk and her victory and her elevation to the role of queen. With her new position, she sent him clothes and money, and he came around the palace daily and sat while her ladies-in-waiting would bring him tidbits of news and carry to her messages from home. When Haman's plan began to circulate in the isolated Jewish community, Mordecai hurried to get word to Esther so she would intervene on her people's behalf. I wonder if he was struck with a tiny bit of amnesia. Had the boy really forgotten that she was "passing" because of his advice?

Well, Sister-girl had really gotten into her new elevated status as queen. She had plush surroundings and closets filled with new clothes. She had no housework and many women to do her every bidding. She had respect and time to enjoy her new space and to revel in being in "the right place." She wasn't concerned with the economic plight of the Jews; all she had to do was make a request, and what she wanted appeared. Why be involved in their lack of land ownership? Look at where she lived. So what that they had no political clout? Hadn't she pulled herself up by her own sandal straps to become queen? If she could move out of the ghetto, so could they!

Her attitude was certainly not one of a bodacious woman. It was the attitude of one who felt she had arrived. But the plight of the Jews did involve her, and one day Mordecai sent her this word: "Esther, don't think that just because you are the queen, you are separate from the consequences before us. You are a Jew, and the Jews are the chosen people of God, whether we tell others, hide it, or even deny it. God is going to save the Jews. If you choose not to intervene, God will still raise up a Savior. Perhaps, Esther, you are in the palace today for such an occasion as this" (4:14). Girlfriend got the clue. Sista got the message. She remembered who she was and whose she was!

Are you aware that few of the businesses in black communities are owned by blacks? Many are owned by members of other racial-ethnic groups. This means that we have little political and economic power, even in our own communities. Yet we have been in America longer than most of the other racial-ethnic communities and have had to work harder with no monetary compensation. The black church is one of the very few buildings that we own in our neighborhoods!

So can we really afford to sit in the building on Sunday only and leave it empty the balance of the week? The thief is in our community, and we have forgotten who we are!

It's time for us to choose sides. Either we work for the thief or we work for the One who comes to bring abundant life. I refuse to rob my own folks. I refuse to hold what I have been blessed with and not to share it with those who are less fortunate. I will not sit by, idle, while the mayhem and violence in our community continue. Because I remember whose I am and where my blessings come from, I am more than willing to support the ministries of my local congregation as we provide hope, nurture, possibilities, and a future for our people. We need every type of ministry to be included inside the church for those outside our walls. We are responsible to them and for them. "They" are the only reason a church exists! If we are not reaching out, touching their lives, and bringing them in, our community dies, bit by bit. And it's our fault. If our communities are taken by the thief, we have helped give it away!

Although the name of God is not mentioned in the entire book of Esther, we know it was the hand of God that intervened. The psalmist, in reflecting upon the plan for the total eradication

of the Jews, says: "If it had not been the Lord
who was on our side, when our enemies attacked
us, then they would have swallowed us up alive.
. . . Blessed be the Lord, who has not given us as
prey to their teeth" (124:2–6). Friends, we have
escaped, and our help is yet in the hands of the
same God. It wasn't until Esther remembered who
she was that God used her as a willing vessel for
salvation. And when we remember, bodacious
women, change will come our way.

Haman was killed on the very gallows he had
prepared for Mordecai. Now that's justice! My
grandma used to tell me whenever I began to wish
harm for someone else, "Gal, when you dig a
ditch, you'd better dig two, one for them and the
other for you." Grandma was a smart old girl.
Haman had been so very sure that he was going
to kill the Jews. Haman had been so very positive that his plan was fail-safe. Haman had gotten the king to endorse his wickedness and felt
that he was "sho nuff the man." But, Esther called
the Jews to fast and pray. Esther remembered that
they were people of the covenant. Esther remembered that they had untold help in the Maker of
heaven and earth. She didn't know how God
would intervene, but she knew that somehow
God would.

The Reverend Carroll Felton, a bold black brother and a mighty man in the pulpit, has gone to be with God. Carroll preached a sermon for my black seminarians' graduation celebration about a "theology of somehow." It helped me put Esther, a bodacious woman of color, in better perspective. Carroll declared that this theology would make you bold and masterful even when you are shy and retiring. It will make you come alive with optimism even when you're surrounded by pessimism. It will stir you with strength when you're faced with weakness. It will convert your confused thinking and shape your defeatist attitude into one of invincible and unshakable determination. When you operate out of a theology of somehow, it brings sanity to an insane world and gives hope to the hopeless in the midst of their struggles. Sister Esther relied on the God of "somehow."

All nature gives credibility to this theology. For we stand in awe and wonder at the creative order of the universe, forever inquiring, "How?" The answer comes back, "Somehow." How is it that the sun knows its appointed time and place? How does the moon control the ebbing tides? The greatest scientist only has a theory, but we know God does it "somehow." How is it that the alarm clock of eternity never fails and the seasons roll in perfect order? How is it that the dewdrops continue to fall in silence and the thunder knows to announce the coming of the rain? I don't know how, but "somehow." How is it that the flowers never forget their fragrance and the morning glory needs no reminder to wake up and open its petals toward heaven at the coming of the sun? How is it that the stars know their time of entrance onto the darkened stage of night and the planets can chart their own course through the universe? I don't know how, but "somehow."

When we finish wrestling with nature and turn to Holy Scripture, it's for sure that Pharaoh's army wanted to know "how" as they felt the waters cover them on a superhighway that had been completely dry. The council at Jericho wanted to know "how" their walls came tumbling down at the off-key notes of a trumpet. The 450 prophets of Baal wanted to know "how" as water soaked the altars at Mount Carmel. And I'm positive that Haman asked "how" as he saw the rope he had hung for Mordecai coming down around his own neck!

Esther stood in a long line of bodacious women who depended on this God of "somehow." Centuries later, early on a Sunday morning before dawn, in a graveyard just outside Jerusalem, some bodacious sisters saw that the stone that had sealed a tomb was now rolled away. When they looked inside and saw that the clothes had been neatly folded in an empty grave, they asked the angels, "How?" I'm sure the response was simply, "Somehow!"

Like Esther, we cannot sit inside the walls of our local churches and accept being a part of a dying system. We must go forward, like Esther, depending on God to lead us in the right path, to provide the right vision, and to bring the right resources our way. For our communities are hurting. The thief of our soul is searching and threatening, seeking others to devour. We must be bodacious women. We must provide help, health, and hope. How? God will work through us, somehow!

What can we do? Where do we start? Where do we begin? We begin when we remember that stewardship is faithful, committed discipleship that is required of each of us. Stewardship is not a campaign. It is not a fund drive. It is not a committee project. Stewardship is our daily response to the love of God that is so freely given unto us. Whatever you have is a trust from God. You are only a steward for God. And you are responsible to multiply what you have in deeds of loving service to your neighbors, who are everywhere.

That brings me to the issue of calling bodacious women to tithe. We must, should, ought be moved so much by the love of God for us that we volunteer to support the ministries of our local church with both our tithe and our gifts of service. We can share in equal sacrifice when we determine to give 10 percent of our income back to God. It makes no difference how much you make on your job; regardless of whether you are on a fixed income or dependent on a welfare check, 10 percent is required of us all! I don't have to answer to anyone about my monthly pledge. I'm not required to finance every dinner, bake sale, or outing. I pay my tithes. I pay them off the top. God has given me the strength to make my salary, so I would not insult God by tithing after Uncle Sam has gotten his share. It makes for easy math, which I need, when I look at my gross and deduct my tithes from it.

Tithing is the only matter in scripture where God challenges us, "Let's make a deal. You give me back 10 percent of what I bless you with, and watch me open the windows of heaven and pour out blessings that you will not have room enough to receive." (Malachi 3:10). Tithing is more than fair, it's equality at its best!

Bodacious women also want to share in the equal work of ministry in their local congregations by being active in some type of outreach with others. We share in equal growth by attending either church school or midweek Bible study. And we come together on Sunday to celebrate our ministry through the week in order to learn more and to do more. Girlfriend, don't you be a thief and decide that what God has blessed you with is yours to keep.

It takes thieves to plot, plan, and determine that without permission, they can take what rightfully belongs to God and God's ministry. It takes thieves to have no regard for violating the work of ministry to satisfy their selfish demands. I don't know how God works despite thieves in the church, but God has a record of doing it "somehow."

The "garage robber" and Haman teach us about the care of God. Often it takes the work of a thief to help us see the goodness, the providence, and the provisions of God. Proverbs 13:22 says, "The wealth of the sinner is stored up for the righteous." I cannot explain how God will take what you have tried to steal and get it back. But I know that the Word works. When you steal from God, the money you stole might go to pay a righteous doctor for your failing heath, or to pay a righteous lawyer for the trouble that comes your way, or even to pay a righteous counselor for your confused thinking about a messed-up relationship. Stealing from God is not worth it, for that stolen money will not be a blessing to you. Give it up!

Just Between Us

- Do you tithe?
- Why or why not?
- Have you been overly generous lately, or are you caught being a "red-handed" thief?
- What have you done with your gifts for the community in the past three months?
- Have you ever been robbed?
- Did it make you angry?
- Did it make you feel violated and vulnerable?
- Have you ever experienced God's making a way for you "somehow"?
- Imagine how God feels when we withhold our tithes, our time, and our talents or gifts.

- Have you ever, like Esther, tried to "pass" for someone or something you were not?
- What were the consequences of forgetting your roots?
- Is your local church standing empty and unused all week?
- What are the needs you see in your community?

Suggestions

Girlfriend, this is serious business! Regardless of what your reason or excuse might be for not giving God a minimum 10-percent tithe, make up your mind that you will try God's "let's make a deal" plan for the next thirty days. To not tithe is to rob yourself, for whatever you give God as a tithe is only an investment that will pay big dividends for you. God doesn't need your money, but you surely need God to increase what you get.

Being poor or being on welfare or being in so much debt is no reason not to allow God to get you up and out of the valley of "don't have" and "can't seem to find." The way up and out is through the avenue of tithing from whatever you receive. Don't be concerned with what the church does with God's money after you give it. Just put it in the offering envelope, and put your name on it for tax purposes, but see it as your investment with God, not with the finance committee, the administrators, or the pastor. They can't play "let's make a deal" with you. This is strictly between you and God. After thirty days, if it doesn't work, call God a liar!

chapter twelve

~

LESSONS IN FINDING
A MIGHTY GOOD MAN

Song of Solomon 1:6

The story is told that in Africa, the price for a
new bride was once two cows. When a man had
serious intentions about marriage, he had to ar-
range to purchase two healthy, well-fed cows to
present to the father of the bride. In a certain
village lived an ugly woman who had three beautiful sisters. The sisters had been married and their
bride price had been paid, but there had never
been an inquiry about the ugly woman's avail-
ability by the marriage maker of the village. The
woman's parents decided to publicize the fact that
they would pay up to four cows to any man who
would take their ugly daughter as a bride. They
felt she would do well with the work and chores
of marriage. Ugliness would not affect her pro-
ductivity.

Of course, the woman became the laughing-stock of the village: "She's so ugly that her family has to pay!" The story of the ugly woman traveled from village to village as her self-esteem was slaughtered, her self-confidence failed, and her hopes for a family withered and died. But one day, a stranger appeared at the door, asking for her father. He was from many villages away and had come with a proposition. The father came to meet their guest with a staunch determination not to pay more than four cows for his daughter. Was he ever surprised when the guest offered to pay him eight cows for the woman! The father, being an honorable man, wanted him to see the woman, who was no longer young. The husband-to-be did not choose to embarrass the woman further and said to her father that the price of eight well-fed, healthy cows would be delivered the next morning and he would like to have the marriage arranged.

Needless to say, this arrangement was the talk of the town. Both men and women wondered about the craziness of a man who would pay such an unheard-of price for a woman they all knew to be so ugly that her parents had been willing to pay him. In that village he was denounced as a fool, a crazy man, even an idiot. But early the next morning, the cows arrived, the man came back, the marriage ceremony was performed, and the ugly woman left as a bride.

The marriage thrived, for the ugly daughter was never brought or sent back home. Many beautiful women had their feelings hurt, and many nights there was quarreling in the village tents as husbands were asked, "Was I not worth eight cows to you?"

The wise and the otherwise pondered this situation, and as the history of the village was compiled by the griot (storyteller), the story of the bride worth eight cows became legend. Many years later, a new griot decided that this tale was worth a follow-up, and he decided to travel the many miles to see how this particular marriage had gotten along. After many days of walking and searching, he was directed to the home of the couple.

A beautiful woman responded. He was thinking this was the housekeeper or even a second or third wife. He inquired whether this was the home of the man who had paid a bride price of eight cows. The woman replied yes. The reporter asked if he might speak with the husband, and the woman went to get him. The reporter did not know how to ask the question, "How could you have been so stupid as to pay an unheard-of price for an ugly woman?" for one did not insult a man inside his own home. So when the husband entered the room and made him welcome, the reporter simply asked, "For the record, please tell me why you did it."

Immediately, the husband asked, "Did not my wife let you in the house?" The reporter replied, "Your young and beautiful wife allowed me entrance." "Well, did you not think she was worth even ten cows?" challenged the husband. The reporter of course replied, "Yes. But I am not questioning why you would pay ten cows for a beautiful woman. I have traveled this distance to understand why you paid eight cows for an ugly woman." The husband was quiet for a few minutes. Then he called for his wife. The very beautiful and gracious woman entered the room. The husband introduced her to the storyteller. "This is my only wife. She is the one I paid eight cows for and would gladly pay eight more. She has made my life complete, and I knew she would."

The reporter cried, "They said she was ugly!" "She was never ugly," the husband said. "Her beauty is on the inside, never just shown on her face. Before we married, she was simply a reflection of what she was told. They said she was ugly. They treated her as if she was ugly. And she behaved in response. They took her self-esteem, her pride, and her self-confidence. But eight cows told her a different story. Eight cows made a great difference in how she thought about herself and how she carried herself. In all of our land, no other woman ever had that amount paid for her. My wife knew that I didn't think or feel that she was ugly. And you are a witness. She is not ugly! I'm glad I could see beneath the surface, for look at what a treasure I have."

Friends, the absence of loving attitudes and loving practices is at the root of most of the ugliness in our world. Most of us grew up feeling that there was something wrong with us, something missing, something incomplete. These feelings make us believe that we are unworthy of pure love. We don't think we deserve love that we don't have to search for, struggle with, and earn to keep. But that's a lie. It's a myth that we have brought into our lives and that has made life miserable for ourselves and others. For love is our source. The domain of love is within each one of us. It is in the stillness of your own heart where you must first go to find and experience true love. For there is the divine image within each one of us, which is the love of God. This makes us worthy of all that God has in store for bodacious women. This is the holy presence that should draw all things good and beautiful into our world. This is the creative source from which we should live, develop, and expand our fullest potential. For the realm of love is within, and beauty grows from the inside out. Yet most of us have been taught that we are not worth four cows! This low self-esteem, low self-confidence, and low expectation allows us to accept too little, take too much, and cheat ourselves of the love we rightly deserve.

The Song of Solomon is a book about the love between a man and a woman. Many say that it is the love story of King Solomon and a black Shulammite woman, who tells him in 1:6: "Do not gaze at me because I am dark, because the sun has gazed on me. My mother's sons were angry with me; they made me keeper of the vineyards, but my own vineyard I have not kept!" Oh, the story of the American black woman! Ours is the tale of women who take care of everyone else at their own expense. Some say the Song of Solomon is about sensual, sexual love. Others say it is a story about God and God's love for Israel, the church. Whatever school of thought you choose to believe, it yet remains that this one book of the Bible speaks in detail about the intimate relationship of love, marriage, and sex. This book is clear that God feels that love, sex, and marriage are all important elements in our lives. Here is modeled a loving relationship, physical and emotional longings, and the experience of pleasure and joy, all within the framework of marriage and commitment.

This book is a historical story that we can read on two levels. On the human level, we can learn much about love, marriage, and sex. On another level, we can experience God's overwhelming love for us. This book was included in the canon of Scripture so that the people of God might have a wedding song honoring marriage, promoting courtship, and detailing the intimacy that must exist between a man and a woman who love each other. This book makes clear that the two individuals ought both be equal in their love for God and in their love for each other. This book clearly says to the church that sexual escapades between priest or preacher and members is not God's ideal. Secret rendezvous and extramarital affairs adopted in today's immoral climate are not sanctioned by God. We live in a day when sex has been twisted, exploited, and turned into urgent, illicit, casual, and self-gratifying activities that do not please God, bring ruin into our homes, and cause our children to run around imitating our ungodly behavior.

But, bodacious woman, the Word of God confronts us, and I want to engage this text to see with what type of man we should be willing to enter into a relationship that would lead to marriage and procreation. For I am concerned about relationships that cause so many of us pain, hurt, agony, and loneliness. I am very much in touch with the reality that we often put ourselves on the line for men who mean us no good, who come into our lives only to take what they can and then leave when the cost becomes too much for them. I have lived the reality of a man who is fine, has all the exterior trappings, and then, when the babies begin to grow up, decides that he does not want to be a responsible man. And I know the experience of looking for a tall, dark, and handsome man, only to run into a short, slight, light-complexioned man who is the mighty man in my life today.

I learned the difference the old-fashioned way, by trial and error. I learned by making the mistake of looking at the outside and not checking out the inner substance. And today, I am committed to teaching what I have learned, both in the halls of academia and in the school of hard knocks and broken hearts. So today, as a woman, a sister, a wife, a mother, and a pastor called by God, I declare unto you that God has some principles for bodacious women to use to find their mighty men:

Principle 1. Seek a man who can discern the inner you, one who can read your eyes and not just your made-up face.

Principle 2. Seek a man who knows personal struggle and can articulate his story.

Principle 3. Seek a man who has a dream and a plan to achieve it.

Principle 4. Seek a man who loves God and is active in his local congregation. Find one who can't always visit your church because of his involvement in his own!

Principle 5. Seek a man with a reputation you can verify, someone who's known by his good deeds.

Principle 6. Seek a man who's willing to wait, someone with experience in delayed gratification.

Principle 7. Seek a man who has good, healthy family relationships, especially with his mother, aunts, and sisters. The way he treats these women speaks volumes about how he will treat you.

Principle 8. Seek a man who is competitive in giving and generous in nature.

Principle 9. Seek a man who has proven to be stable, has a home or apartment, a job, a car. What has he finished? What has he accomplished?

Principle 10. Seek a man who has obvious pride in his achievements, dress, and self, one who has race consciousness and respect for elders.

When you find a man this good, you know you have found a godly man, a born-again, Holy Spirit-filled individual. Until you find him, wait on God. Don't rush ahead of God. Don't get in a hurry. Don't settle for "breath and britches." Wait. He's also searching for you. Wait. He's in another village, and he's being instructed by God to get the bride price ready. He knows that you are worth more than eight cows. He's on the way. Wait!

You'll know him, for you can lay his résumé side by side with Jesus'. You'll know him, for he will be cut from the same mold and will have the same attributes. This is reason enough for not being unequally yoked with an unbeliever. Unbelievers can look good. Unbelievers can talk well. Unbelievers can have the outer trappings of job, car, and dress. But unbelievers don't have the staying power that comes with Christ. Unbelievers can't go the long run with you; they are simply sprinters. But life and commitment are about running the distance. Unbelievers are fickle, here today and gone tomorrow.

But there are mighty men, those who imitate Christ and have a made-up mind and a determined heart to walk with you through the good times and the bad, through the ups and the downs. They love you when you're beautifully made up, and they'll love you even better when they see what you look like in the morning when you just wake up. A mighty man will love you when your shape is young and slender and will continue to love you when the hips have broadened and the waistline has become thick. A mighty man will love you when your hair is thick and long and will love you just as much when you take it off and hang it on the dresser. For a mighty man knows that your real beauty is on the inside.

Compare your man to a mighty good man whose name is Jesus:

1. Jesus knows all about us and loves us just the same. While we were yet sinners, he died for us, for he saw what we could become.

2. Jesus knew the struggles of racism, sexism, and classism. But one day, by the side of an old well, he touched a woman who was hurting, told her the story of his messiahship, and sent her rejoicing on her way.

3. Jesus went to the wilderness one day to meet a teacher called Satan. He had received a vision from God, and Satan tried to get him to change his mind. But in the wilderness, Jesus formulated his plans for the work of his ministry, and no devil from hell was able to trick him, outslick him, or manipulate his plans to go through the fires of hell for me and you.

4. Jesus loved God so much that he made time with and devotion to God a priority in his life. If God said it, Jesus did it. If God wasn't in it, Jesus wanted no part of it. He sent his posse away to spend time with God. He hid from the seeking crowds to be in communion with God. He would go to the mountains, to the desert, and out on a lonely sea just to be in the company of God.

5. People talked about Jesus. His reputation grew until it was said, "He just goes around doing good." He cast out demons, and the

people talked. He healed the sick, and the people talked. He put up with the company of women and children, and people talked. But his reputation grew as he worked to help and to heal.

6. The devil tried to give Jesus easy access to success, but Jesus said, "This world is not my Kingdom, for my Kingdom is not made with hands, but is eternal in the heavens" (John 18:36). The people tried to make him a king, but he slipped away, for the dominion had been given to him by God before the foundation of the world. He knew that he had to work to receive the dominion. He knew he had to give his life as a ransom for our sin. He knew that the gratification of seeing every knee bow and every tongue confess was going to be delayed for generations. But my Savior was willing to wait.

7. Jesus was his mother's son. He escorted her to a wedding at Cana in Galilee and did his first miracle at her request. Then, as he was dying on a cruel and rugged cross, he said, "Woman, behold your son. For, woman, I thank you for bringing me into this cruel world. Woman, I thank you for feeding me, changing me, and caring for me as you do. Woman, I thank you for teaching me how to walk, talk, and be part of an earthly family.

So, John, take care of my mother!" (John 19:26–27). He cared for her even in his dying.

8. Jesus was competitive in giving away all that he possessed until the very end. He began by giving the disciples his power and sending them out on a mission two by two. Then, he promised the disciples that even "when I go away, I will not leave you comfortless. When I am gone away, I'm going to send you another Comforter, who will lead you and guide you in all Truth"(John 14:26). Jesus was generous to a fault. He gave and gave until he gave up his life and cried out, "It is finished!" (John 19:30).

9. What did Jesus finish? What did he accomplish? Well, look at your own life. Check out your own history. Not only did he die on Calvary, but he rose again to help us rise from the places we used to live. The things we used to do, we don't do anymore. Because of his work in our lives, there has been a great change. And he's not through with us yet. We can rise higher still, because one Easter morning, he got up, finished with death, borrowed graves, and hell.

10. Talk about pride! The story has been circulated that when Jesus returned to

heaven, one of the angels met him at the gate and inquired about his earthly mission. "Why did you let them hurt you? Why did you let them betray you? Why did you let them kill you? You could have called a million angels, and we would have come." Jesus didn't say a word. So, the angel went on. "What about your mission strategy for continuing? Do you realize that there is no mass media to spread your word? There are no cables, faxes, or even televisions to take your message far and wide. What in the world is going to happen to this effort for which you let them take your life? Jesus looked down the corridors of time and said, "I left them my name. I can depend on them."

Bodacious Woman, even the Child of God is waiting for you to get what you deserve, and it ain't about a second-class, worthless good-for-nothing. For Girlfriend, you are worth more than even ten cows. Jesus gave his life for you, and that makes you invaluable! That makes you priceless! And it makes you worth the long trip that the right man is taking to get to you. Hold on—what God's got for you is on the way!

Just Between Us

- Have you been feeling ugly lately?
- How many cows do you feel you are worth?
- Have you been working in or tending your own garden, or have you been busy taking care of everybody else's garden?
- What did your mama teach you about self-care?
- What did you learn by watching her own self-tending?
- What are you teaching the daughters who are watching you?
- How does your significant other rate on the "principles list"?
- What does this score say about you?
- What do the Scriptures say about you and your value?
- Could God possibly want more for you than you've accepted so far?

Suggestions

Take time to sit with a few "soul sistas" and talk about the list of principles. Be honest as you assess what more you need from the mighty man in your life. If you have a mighty man, set aside some significant period of time to say "thanks" in special ways. Mighty men are hard to find. Consider yourself mighty fortunate if your blessing has already arrived. If you are waiting for him to make it to your village, what do you need to be busy doing for yourself to be prepared when he arrives? If you are raising a potential mighty man (son, grandson, or nephew), make sure that you instill loving, ethical values, and appreciation for what you are providing him now.

chapter thirteen

GOD'S LOVE AFFAIR WITH A WHORE

Book of Hosea

When a new preacher came to town, everybody talked about how good she was and how much better she was than the old preacher. The town skeptic inquired with interest of one of the trustees, what this new woman was preaching that made her so different from the old one. "Well, the old preacher told us we were all lost sinners and unless we repented we were all going to hell," was the reply. The skeptic asked, "And what does this new preacher say?" "This new preacher tells us that we are all lost sinners and unless we repent we are all going to hell," was the reply. The skeptic said, "I can't tell the difference." The trustee answered, "Oh, there's a big difference. This preacher says it with tears in her eyes!"

This is, of course, the mark of a true prophet. For as a mouthpiece of God makes judgments and pronounces warning, it's always with a heavy heart and tears. The tears, like the words, are those of our God. For God yearns to be in relationship with us. So, long ago and far away, God selected one who would cry because of God's longing for us, one who would cry as he told us of God's deep love for us. And, to make the tears genuine and authentic, God chose Hosea and set him in a relationship that was doomed before it began.

Hosea was sent to the harlots' district. Hosea's heart was fixed on a well-built, finely designed, nicely groomed, and sweet-smelling woman who made her living by selling her body. She was desirable. She knew the language of love. She had the right moves. She knew the sweet talk. She had learned the seductive walk. And she won Hosea's heart. The man of God, the mouthpiece of God, fell in love with a bodacious woman who was a prostitute.

Poor Hosea. He didn't want to buy a few stolen moments of her time. He wanted to be with her. He proposed marriage, the ultimate joining of two souls. He took the prostitute to the Temple. In the age-old custom, they looked each other in the eyes and pledged to love each other, to be faithful to each other, and to honor each other as husband and wife. Then they left the altar and went home to the marriage bed.

Hosea treated Gomer royally, but it wasn't enough. Hosea loved her faithfully, but it wasn't enough. One day as he went to Temple out the front door, she slipped away out the back door. Gomer didn't need money, fine clothes, or security, but the girl wanted excitement! So, in spite of the marriage vows, she began to whore, giving herself away to different lovers.

I would imagine that the first time this bodacious woman had an affair, she returned home filled with guilt. That first affair with reckless living is always heady and intoxicating. It gives a sense of getting away with something. Cheating is fun! Even the Bible records in Proverbs 9:17, "Stolen waters are sweet, and bread eaten in secret is pleasant." But when you've cheated and not gotten caught, it doesn't take away the inner guilt. So, that first affair after the marriage found Gomer treating Hosea extra special. She was extra nice. She was mighty sweet. She gave herself away by pretending too much. Hosea didn't say a word, and the slipping away into her former style of living continued.

But all sin has its consequences. What is done in secret will be shouted from the rooftops, admonishes Luke 12:2–3, and Gomer's affairs caught up with her at least three distinct times.

For she got pregnant. In the days of Hosea and
Gomer, both the wife and the children were property of the husband. Names were not trivial pursuits taken from a book but had religious meaning to symbolize a particular truth about the infant. God had Hosea name the first child, a son,
Jezreel, meaning "punishment is coming." The
second child, a daughter, was named Lo-
ruhamah, "no love shown." And the third child,
another son, was named Lo-ammi, or "no longer
my people."

The jig was up! There was no longer any reason for slipping and sliding. After the weaning
of the third child, Gomer left and returned openly
to her former life. And when you have left the
sweet, clean tenderness of a loving relationship
to go in search of excitement and fulfillment,
there is no place to go but down. For living apart
from real love will destroy the very essence of who
you were created to become. Like all bodacious
women, Gomer had been searching for the real
thing. She had wanted to be part of the crowd.
Gomer wanted something different from the rou-
tine ritual of day-to-day living as a wife and
mother, so she turned her back on her vows.

Some folks were happy to see her back in the

mix. Some laughed at Hosea for being such a fool in the first place. Some men asked for her simply because she had been the wife of God's spokesperson. But this type of life is not easy. This type of living pulls you down. And Gomer's beauty began to fade. The wrinkles began to come. The tension began to wreak havoc upon her mind, body, and spirit. The years were not kind. And Girlfriend couldn't do what she used to do, like she used to do it. Money got thin, and friends got few. Hair and teeth come out without proper care. The body gives way without proper nutrition and treatment. As the songwriter says, "Nobody wants you when you're down and out." Yet Hosea wanted her. Hosea yearned for her. Hosea even cried for her. To him, she was yet a bodacious woman.

God waited until Gomer was in the garbage dump, foraging for food and just barely surviving, and when she thought her end was near, God sent Hosea to bring her back home. Can you imagine her thoughts when she saw him? She knew what she was. She was no longer a prostitute, selling her body to different lovers. She had become a whore who gave herself away. And now, nobody wanted what she had left to offer. Her self-esteem was no more. Her self-confidence was gone. She felt that she was both unlovely and unlovable. But here came her husband.

Hosea took his bodacious woman home, for he could see her only through his eyes of love. He didn't see her as a loose woman who left him and the children. She was his wife and she needed him. He picked her up gently and carried her back where she belonged. He ordered her a new wig to cover the places where she had pulled her hair out trying to figure out how to make it day by day. He ordered the dentist to come in and repair her mouth, so that the smile he remembered of her youth could be restored. He ordered the best purple silks and linens. He bought the most costly perfumes and had a maid attend to the body that had been neglected for so long. And when all was ready, he entered her chamber to make love to this whore.

Oh, I'm not talking about simple sex. The boy made love to the girl! He looked deeply into her eyes and told her about the light of love. He whispered sweet nothings into her ears. He played gently with her hair and blew softly upon her lips. He stroked her arms and her fingers. He delighted in the beauty he saw in her body, which she had misused. But Hosea let her know that it didn't matter, for he loved her in spite of what she'd done. He made love to her feet, for it was her mind that had done the planning, but it was her feet that had carried her back into her sin and destruction. Can you see him playing with her toes, caressing them one by one? "This little piggy went to market, this little piggy stayed home. This little piggy had roast beef, this little piggy had none. And this little piggy cried 'Wee, wee, wee' all the way home." The woman knew she was loved. The woman knew she was forgiven. The bodacious woman knew she was restored to her former place of dignity and love. How? Because Hosea made love to her with tears in his eyes!

Now, many folks say this is a myth. Surely God wouldn't do Hosea like this. Many say it's an allegory, not a historical account. But it really doesn't make any difference whether you believe it really happened, for its job is to make us think of how we backslide and whore around on the One who provides everything for us. It's purpose is to make us think of how God yearns to be in relationship with us even when we are at our lowest moral point. It's to make us reflect on how God feels when everything is offered to us and yet we leave God in search of excitement. It's to make us think of how God sent Jesus to cry over us, give his life for us, and offer us hope in a new relationship. God sent Jesus to reach us, my friends. Jesus is the only one who can win us back from the garbage pile of life. Love made a fool out of Hosea in this story. Churchmen and churchwomen down through the ages have played God for the fool, yet God's reckless love continues to cry for us, to take us back time after time. God is yearning for the whore's return today. And this, my sisters, is mighty good news!

Just Between Us

- Have you ever been to the red-light district in your town?
- Have you ever been personally involved with a "woman of the night"?
- Did you ever stop to consider why they're in business?
- Did you ever stop to think about what they could be doing without the men who purchase their services?
- When you are not blessed by your job and aren't a blessing on your job, you are prostituting your God-given gifts. Think about that!

⤚ Is your church involved in any type of ministry to hurting women who attend worship?

Suggestions

Prostitutes were usually victims of incest, rape, or sexual abuse in their youth. Many of them are working mothers. Some are homeless or runaways. Once a month, fill a decorated shoe box with hotel-size lotions, soaps, perfume samples, lipsticks, good books, magazines, and some "light" Christian materials (such as *The Upper Room, Alive Now!,* or *Daily Bread*), and go visit, talk, and share with your sisters. Let them know how much God loves them through your deeds of kindness. Do it with tears in your eyes!

≈

chapter fourteen

HOW DO WE SAY GOODBYE?

John 11:1–44

God knows how very hard it is to say goodbye.
Grief, anger, confusion, dismay, pain, and suffering are involved when you have to let go and
bid farewell. Most of us don't deal very well with
separations. Most of us don't handle parting and
leave-taking with skillful style. Even when it's
someone or something that we don't especially
care for, there is still some anxiety about termi-
nating a relationship. Yet letting go, releasing, and
separating are normal parts of everyday living.
We have accepted the realities of saying hello,
welcome, and greetings. But God knows how very
hard it is for us to say goodbye.

I remember trying to say goodbye to my
mama. More than ten years ago, on May 18, she
had a massive stroke. There was a long surgery
and many long hours of waiting to see if she
would revive from her deep coma. My family

gathered. Her eight children, me and my siblings; her two brothers; her mother who had birthed her and her aunt who had raised her from age eight—we were all there. We sat and talked. We cried. We waited. And we prayed. Mama was hooked to every kind of machine. They pumped, they hummed, they bleeped, and they signaled her vital signs. She hovered between life and death, between earth and heaven. We cried. We waited. We prayed:

> God, if you love her, heal her. God, if
> you love us, bring her back to us. God,
> she loved you, she trusted you, she taught
> us to love you. She had just returned
> from church, worshiping you, when the
> stroke occurred. Where were you, God?
> Do you care, God? We need her, God!
> Do you hear our prayers, God? Where are
> you?

For ten days, we stayed in the hospital lounge. We took turns, split shifts to ensure that she was never alone. We were straining, hoping, wishing to see some improvement, looking for any small progress, waiting for a miracle. We were looking for Jesus. We were crying out for a Savior. We were praying to a God who didn't respond.

Have you ever been there? Have you ever had to stand at the bedside of a dying loved one? had to wonder about a wayward child? had to be concerned about an uncaring, unkind, and insensitive lover or spouse? been overwhelmed about your job being phased out? had to wonder how the pile of debts would get paid or where food for the next meal would come from? had a Christmas coming, with small children and no way to make it a merry one? The problems and losses of our lives will drive us to seek divine intervention. When the pressures mount in our lives, day and night our tears and our prayers will be raised before an all-seeing and all-knowing God. Have you ever tried to pray but could only cry?

There come those times in life when our spirits are troubled and we are weighed down with grief. Often it feels that we are talking to the walls and that our life and its cares are invisible and inconsequential to a God who holds the whole world in the hollow of great hands. Have you ever felt that even God had abandoned you? Talk about being made to feel insignificant! When there is nothing solid about your existence, when chaos and confusion are everywhere, when you call out faithfully to God but get no answer, when you seek mercy from above but see no change in your circumstances, you begin to wonder if God can really provide a balm for broken hearts and a salve for wounded spirits.

I don't know if you comprehend what I'm talking about. But the time came when I got exhausted with trying to tell God about what we needed and how Mama was depending upon the resources of heaven alone. I couldn't sing the songs of victory. I didn't want to read the story of a faithful God. I tried to lift my arms, but they felt like lead. I tried to open my mouth, but my tongue felt like brass. I tried to open my heart and feel for others who were suffering, but I felt that God had rejected us, had forgotten about us, and had left us in this horrible nightmare alone. "Why us?" we cried. There was no response. "How much more?" we inquired, and Mama's brain wave activities started to diminish. "How long?" we begged, and her vital signs began to slow down and become erratic. Yet we stood around her bed, waiting, seeking, longing. We had the firm assurance that God had come so many times before on behalf of the oppressed and the heavy-burdened. We knew God to be the God who comes when we hunger and thirst. So we just stood and waited on God.

This is the story of two bodacious women, Mary and Martha, as they watched their brother, Lazarus, get worse and worse. Martha's house was the one where Jesus and the disciples often came and were refreshed by her wonderful hospitality. It was here where Mary sat at his feet in adoration and worship. It was this same adoring Mary who anointed his head with oil, like the high priest, and signified that he was the Messiah that the world had been awaiting. It was this same worshiping Mary who covered his feet with her tears and wiped them away with her hair. These bodacious women had a relationship with Jesus. These sisters felt they could depend upon Jesus. This family had sent word to Jesus, saying, "Listen, the man you love, our brother, is sick." They just knew that Jesus would come and heal him. They were assured that Jesus would hurry and come with a miracle of restoration. In their hearts they were convinced that Jesus would be right there as soon as their message was received. So they waited. They anticipated his arrival. They expected him to arrive momentarily. For God knows how hard it is to say goodbye.

Jesus got the message. Jesus heard their prayer request. Jesus was well aware of the desire of their hearts. But verses 5–6 say, "Jesus loved Martha, Mary, and Lazarus. So, when he heard that he was sick, he stayed two more days in the place were he was." What kind of business is this, a loving friend who knows your dilemma yet intentionally delays coming to see about you? After four days, Jesus said, in verse 7, "Now, let us go to Judea." The disciples tried to warn him that the Jews had already sought to stone him to death, and they asked him, "And are you going there again?" (v. 8). With his face set for death, with his mind made up to win our salvation, and with the goal of conquering sin, death, and hell, Jesus said to them, "Our friend Lazarus has fallen asleep, but I am going there to awaken him" (v. 11).

Verses 14–15 say that Jesus plainly said, "Lazarus is dead. And, I am glad for your sakes that I was not there, that you may believe. Nevertheless, let us go to him." Four days late, four days after the fact, four days after the man had died, Jesus, the life-giver, took off to answer the sisters' prayer request. The Jews at that time felt that the spirit stayed in a dead body for up to three days and that perhaps resuscitation could occur in that period. To make sure they recognized the glory of God, Jesus deliberately waited for four days. He was four days late, yet he knew that he was right on time. For he may not come when you want him, but he is always on time! He might not come in your time frame, but whenever he arrives on the scene, it's the right time. He might not come according to the ticking of your clock, but heaven and earth operate on his time, as he prepares to come and see about you and your pressing need. He might not show up on time, but he's always *in* time to change your life, to answer your prayer, and to allow God's glory to shine in the bleakest time of your life.

There are no unanswered prayers, my sisters. Your answer is on the way. The answer may be, "Yes, right away." The answer may be, "No, not ever." But more than likely, the answer is, "Wait!" Martha and Mary had to learn how to wait even as they had to learn how to say goodbye. Verse 17 says that when Jesus arrived, Lazarus had been in the tomb for four days. The mourners were there. The sightseers were there. The nosy and the concerned were there. For death always draws a crowd. And Martha ran to Jesus with my words and your words. She came out with accusations: "If you had just been here, my brother would not have died" (v. 21). What she wanted to know was, "Where were you? What took you so long? Didn't you get the message? Why were you messing around? Look at what you've done. It's your fault that my brother is dead!"

Jesus understood her pain and grief. Jesus knew all about her hurting heart. Jesus had a real comprehension of her anxieties and her fears over separating from one who had been there for her, one whom she had grown to love and whom she did not want to release to the cold and final grip of death. So Jesus spoke to her heart, not to her ears. In verses 25–26, Jesus declares, "I am the resurrection and the life. The one who believes in me, though they die, shall live. And whoever lives and believes in me, shall never die. Do you believe this Miss Martha?" And Martha gives one of the first affirmations of faith in verse 27: "Yes, Lord, I believe that you are the Christ, the Son of God, who is to come into the world." Then she ran away secretly to call Mary.

Mary, who anointed him as Messiah and Savior, came with the same accusation as her sister: "Lord, if you had been here, my brother would not have died" (v. 32). The Bible says that when Jesus saw this woman of faith weeping and when he heard her accusation, he groaned in his spirit and was troubled. For Jesus recognized that everybody couldn't understand who he was. But here was one who had thirsted and hungered after his teachings. Here was one who had defied convention and sat at his feet with the men to learn all that he taught. Yet this faith-filled disciple doubted his ability to reign over death. Friends, this is why Jesus wept! Don't you ever let anybody else tell you that Jesus wept with grief over the death of Lazarus. What makes Jesus weep is our unbelief!

If God is to be God anywhere, it is in the face of death. If God is to conquer anything, it has to be the finality of death. Psychology can deal with our depression. Pep talks can fill us with optimism. Prosperity can take away our physical hunger. But there is only one who can deal with our ultimate concern of death. So God, standing in Jesus at the tomb of his beloved friend, was angry at death. God in Jesus at the tomb of Lazarus was actually standing in the enemy's territory, about to put his feet on the head of the serpent and crush him. For death had violated one of God's creations. Death and the grave had imprisoned another Adam. So Jesus stood there smelling the stench of death, ready to defy this ex-archangel and to expose him as the impostor that he has always been. Life stood in death's domain, the cemetery, and began to pray.

In verse 40, Jesus asks those standing with him, "Did I not say that if you would believe you would witness the glory of God?" And when the stone had been rolled away from the entrance of the tomb, Jesus lifted up his voice and began to pray: "God, I thank you that you have heard me. And, I know that you always hear me. But, because of these people who are standing around, the skeptics, and the doubters and the unbelievers, I say this that they may believe you sent me." Life was about to confront death. Life was about to show the power of the Resurrection. Life was about to cross over the great canyon that separates the dead from those with everlasting life.

The wind stopped blowing, and the birds hushed their singing. The clouds couldn't move, and the trees refused to sway. Every eye was focused, and every ear was on full alert. The only sound in the garden was that of a snake slithering fast, trying to get out of sight. Jesus called with a loud voice, "Lazarus, come forth!" And death had to turn him loose. The grave had to let him go. Verse 44 declares, "And, he who had died came out bound, hand and foot with graveclothes, and his face was wrapped with a cloth." The power of God reigned over sin, death, and hell. The authority of everlasting life was evidenced in a graveyard. The supremacy of the Giver of Life was glorified by one who had come four days late! For God knows how difficult it is to say goodbye.

In verse 44, Jesus gives the crowd instructions: "Jesus said to them, 'loose him and let him go.'" These are the directions for saying goodbye. You have to release people, places, and things and let them be free. When something is over, past and gone, complete and done with, if you keep it wrapped up, packaged tightly, and held close, it will stink and continue to decay. Have you ever seen somebody who refuses to let yesterday go? Have you ever been around people who cannot stop living in the past? Their conversation is always about what used to be. "Used to" gets old, for "used to" is dead. And after a while, "used to" starts to stink to everyone who is around it.

Lazarus had died. Lazarus had finished his course. Lazarus had begun a new existence as memory and future hope. He had been wrapped in grave clothes and was bound for his new reality. When Jesus came and spoke new life into a formerly dead body, Lazarus was stinking from the stench of decay. And as much as Jesus was able to do, he didn't perform the miracle of releasing Lazarus for another new beginning. He told the people to do it for themselves. For Jesus knew how hard it is for us to say goodbye to the old.

Too many of us, myself included, want to sit forever at the grave of a loved one, for the body that we knew is all that we can comprehend. We want things to remain the same. We don't want them to change. We don't want to accept difference, variance, or transformation. So we hold on to the body image that we knew. We glorify the portrait of this body in our mind. We grip the idol that is familiar to us. But Jesus says we have to loose it and let it go. If we hold it, it starts to stink. If we hold it, putrefaction sets in. If we hold it, rot and decomposition are its only destiny. We are told to release it and let it go.

Some of us have to let go of old grudges that we have held on to for too long. The division in many local congregations is about what type of music we should sing. Jesus says, "Loose it and let it go." The image we have that a "good" man has to be in charge, in control as overseers and gatekeepers, has a distinct odor of death. Jesus says, "Loose it and let it go." Too many of us belong to the "power broker club" that has always run things, almost into the ground. Our refusal to allow in anything that is fresh, challenging, and life-giving is the stench of rotting flesh. Jesus says, "Loose it and let it go." The habit of holding on to the old, living out of the past, and always bringing up former ghosts, dragging out their shadows, and pulling around their dead spirits has held too many of us in a graveyard mentality for too long. Jesus says, "Loose it and let it go."

Bodacious woman, you're in the cemetery. Bodacious woman, you are in a confrontation with death. Bodacious woman, the choice of new life is before you. Jesus says this day, you have to loose the past and let it go. You have to begin to look toward tomorrow. You have to get a fresh vision of yourself as a daughter of the Most High God. You have to move out of the graveyard of "used to." You have to let go of "what we have always done." You have to turn loose of "we have never done it that way before."

Jesus said, "Loose it and let it go." You have heard this before. You continue to say, "I want to hold on to the old ways and stay in this graveyard and wait on a new Jesus, a new Savior, a new voice." But, in his mercy and with his loving-kindness, Jesus has come again to plead with you, "Loose the old and let it go."

Ten years ago, my family had to gather at my mother's bedside. Both of her mothers and all of her children were there. We gathered around and individually told her how much we loved her and what she meant to us. We joined hands and prayed for her journey into eternity and new life. And we released her into the capable hands of a loving God. Only one of us had been there to celebrate her first birth, but all of us were there to witness her birth into everlasting life. We had to loose our image of the Mama that we had always known. We had to let go of our portrait of the caring, nurturing, cooking, praying woman and see her as a child of a loving God. We had to take off our expectations and anticipate what God had in store for this woman who had given her life for us. She hadn't been perfect. She had her faults and limitations. There were many things she could have done differently. But she was Mama, and we wanted her to stay with us just the way we knew her. But in letting go of her, we got more of her, for now she is carried in the heart of each one of us. She is not confined to Polk Street in Gary, Indiana. I don't have to pay long-distance charges. I can talk to her anytime I want, for I have accepted her in a new way, as a new being, and she is free. She is a new bodacious woman.

You have to release people so that both of you can grow into your best selves. For when we let go of what used to be, we will be free to embrace the wonderful, new future that God has planned for us. We will never be apart from yesterday anyway, for what has touched your life has changed you, and you can never be the same. Whether you are saying goodbye to an individual you are sad to leave or to one whose leave-taking brings rejoicing and hope for things to return to the way they "used to be" makes no difference. Every contact has touched our lives by the gracious design of Jesus Christ, and there is no going back to yesterday! We will become our very best selves only when we learn to reflect, reminisce, and then let go of what has been and fully engage what is to become.

I know that many of you thirst for a more meaningful relationship with Christ. I know that many of you are thirsting for ways to be connected with the One who supplies life-giving water that can satisfy your soul. I know that many of you are thirsting for ways to touch others and to allow others to touch you. From the cross of Calvary, Jesus cried out for somebody to meet his needs. "I thirst," he said. As he was dying to win our salvation and to ensure our eternal life, the One who was the living water needed someone to give him water to quench his thirst. For, yes, even Jesus had to be aware of how difficult it was to let go of what is familiar in this life.

You need to consent to losing your expectations, letting go of your need for control, and giving up your unrealistic notions that you know more than God. God knows how hard it is to say goodbye to "used to" and yesterday. But the instructions are clear. We have to let go in order that we can let God. Graveyards are not the final stop. Just because the folks met Jesus in the graveyard, they didn't remain there, for Jesus conquered death and brought new life. Jesus gained the victory and turned a weeping crowd into a rejoicing community. Jesus made glad hearts from those that had been sad. Jesus dried tearful eyes and put smiles and laughter on people's faces. Jesus made an example of resurrection out of a man who had been dead for four days. Jesus turned a funeral into a party and put belief into the hearts of many who had doubted him before. He gave them a foretaste of glory divine and let us in on the secret that every closed eye ain't dead! For in Jesus there is always abundant and eternal life, and that is mighty, mighty good news!

Just Between Us

- Do you need to say goodbye to somebody or something from the past?
- Why are you continuing to hold on?
- What benefits are you gaining from not releasing that person or thing?
- What price are you paying for holding on?
- When was the last time you had to say goodbye to a loved one?
- How did you accomplish this?
- Have you ever written a "farewell" letter to someone already dead?
- Have you ever prayed a farewell?
- When was the last time you had to say hello to a new situation?
- How did you do it?

Suggestions

Read Psalm 86 several times. David is praying, lamenting, and grieving about his personal situation. Write your own prayer to God about a painful situation you'd like to let go of now.

chapter fifteen

~

WAITING TO EXHALE
RESURRECTION

Mark 16:1–11, Luke 24:1–10

Once upon a time, four women began their
journey just before the break of day. Each one
was an inquirer. Each one had unnerving questions about the future. Each one was serious about
the journey ahead. They were four women, filled
with fears and anxieties; four women hurt by loss,
stunned by failure, angry about rejection, and fed
up with dashed hopes and broken dreams; four
women with love to give, devotion to offer, and
hearts aching to be fulfilled; four women with
histories of painful experiences, unrealistic expectations, and wounded spirits from roads traveled
too many times before.

Four women were on their way, with no man
in sight. Four women were on their way, with no
"happy ever after" promised. Four women were

on their way, united to empower each other. Four
women were on their way, struggling, wrestling,
and determined to make the journey. They traveled in history. They traveled as community. They
traveled for you and for me. Because they nurtured each other and became midwives to each
other's hopes and dreams, their story is worth
telling. It is a story worth our consideration. It is
a story of the discovery of that very first Easter
Sunday.

This is the story of the love, responsibility, devotion, and intentionally of sisters of color in
Scripture. They were not making this journey out
of overwhelming hope and eager anticipation.
They had no knowledge of an Easter. They had
no awareness of a risen Savior. They had no fore-
sight of an angelic being or an empty tomb. This
was no high, holy, and spiritual trip they were
making. But they were in process, they were
moving forward, they were on their way to see
about a cold, dead corpse.

These bodacious women came to attend to a
body that was already wrapped in a winding-
sheet. They came to do their last act of love for a
dead man. Early, in the dark, before a stream of
sun streaked the sky, they were on their way. They

had had no Holiday Inn or Radisson bed the
night before. No limo service or male escort was
present in this most chilling and frightening hour
of the day. For you do know that the darkest hour
is just before the dawn. But with fragrant spices
and washrags in hand, these sisters were on the
journey.

They were traveling after being in attendance
at the crucifixion. With grieving hearts and hor-
rified eyes, they had witnessed the torture of the
beloved Jesus. They had heard the hammer hit
the nails; they had seen the nails tear his flesh.
The taunts of the crowd had pierced their ears,
and the rupture of his heart had surely broken
theirs. They had been there and had seen with
their own eyes that cruel Roman soldier take a
broad-headed spear and open the fountain in the
Savior's side. For six hours they had stood and
watched Jesus die.

They had been there as the blood of remission
and the water of renewal ran down. They had
watched as the blood for pardon and the water
for purity flowed. They had watched as the blood
for guilt and the water to purge sin streamed forth.
They had watched as the blood for justification
and the water for sanctification joined in sweet

harmony. They had watched as the blood of sacramental wine and the water of baptism mixed to birth the church of the living God.

They had been part of the small funeral. They had seen the empty tomb. They had watched two strong men seal the entrance with a stone at least six feet wide and three feet high. They had observed the law and become the official mourners for this dead Jewish man: "Call for the mourning women; let them come and take up a lament for us" (Jeremiah 9:17). Tired, mourning, grieving, and filled with despair, these bodacious women set off on a serious journey toward a tomb to see about Jesus.

Listen to their question: "Who will roll the stone away for us?" (Mark 16:3). It was a good question, for the stone was a major impediment to the completion of their task. The stone became a stumbling block to the fulfillment of their mission. The stone was no figment of their imagination but a harsh reality they would have to deal with. Yet despite the stone, these sisters were on the journey. Perplexed with speculative difficulty, surrounded by the mysterious unknown, and certain that their own finite capabilities were inadequate, they pressed onward.

The stone was a problem for the future. The

stone would not deter or alter their journey. They
saw themselves already past the stone. They pro-
jected themselves to the other side of this dilemma. They marched on despite their questions,
for they had a united vision of being victorious.
There was a man who needed their ministry and
mission, and no stone would keep them away.

When these first disciples arrived at the tomb,
they found that the stone had already been rolled
away. When the women arrived, seeking a dead
body to take care of, they found a living, angelic
being with a message of hope for them to share.
When the women arrived at the tomb, they witnessed Easter and new life. They had been terri-
fied, afraid, filled with fear, and waiting to exhale, but because they were bodacious women,
they had stayed on the journey. The good news
is that the stone had not been moved to let Jesus
out. The stone had been moved to allow the
women access inside! And the good news for us
is that Jesus keeps rolling stones out of our way.

We have traveled the Christian journey with
our own personal stones. Every one of us has a
"stone story" to share. The stone of pain and grief
fills our spirit. The stone of failure and loneliness
grips our hearts. The stone of wayward children
and restless spouses removes sleep from our

nights. The stone of declining finances and lacka-daisical attitudes about worship makes worry grip our minds. The stone of drugs and alcohol has imprisoned our community. The stone of HIV and AIDS has penetrated our families. The stone of diminishing health and aging limitations holds us in its grasp. But Easter Sunday morning says that Jesus is the master of rolling stones away. Jesus is the authority at stone removal. Jesus is the commander-in-chief of the stone elimination business.

Bodacious women were the very first ones to arrive that morning. We were the witnesses that Jesus had risen and that the Resurrection had oc-curred. We were the ones for whom Jesus rolled the stone away! The stone cannot keep us from Jesus, for he is not locked in behind some sealed tomb. He has already taken care of our stone, so it is left up to us to run and tell the story. Be-cause of our collective memory, we know that we have been left a legacy of being bodacious women. There is biblical history and precedent for our being bodacious women. And, the broken world in which we live is crying out for us to remain bodacious women who continue to change the land. No longer do we have to remain in stag-nant conditions, waiting to exhale! We can meet the risen Christ and be transformed by Jesus' life, filled with the Holy Spirit, and empowered for the days ahead. As Sister Toni Braxton sings it, bodacious women can go on and "breathe again"!

Just Between Us

- Are you still waiting to exhale?
- What do you need to do to breathe again?
- What will it take to make you stop waiting for what may never come?
- Are you tired of the pain and emptiness of unrealistic expectations of what someone male will do for you?
- Have you been looking for love in all the wrong places?
- If you are single, do you recognize that one is a whole number?
- If you are married, do you recognize that a couple is the sum total of two whole ones?
- Have you experienced Easter in your life?
- Have you called in the "stone removal authority" for assistance with your life?
- Have you developed a group of sisters you can count on to walk the long journey with you?

Suggestions

The book is over! The stories of these bodacious women have come to an end. Now it's your turn to make history! Select the one story that stands out as representative of your present situation. Reread it. How is it similar to your situation? How is it different? The main character made some significant choices to affect the outcome. Write a contract with yourself outlining what you will do to make a difference in the next month. Then write down the concrete and specific actions you will have to do each week to arrive at your new destination. Ask God for guidance. Look to Jesus for inspiration. And expect the Holy Spirit to give you the power you need. You are not alone. The Divine Council decreed "in the beginning" that you would be bodacious. You were given power, authority, and dominion, so just go, Girl!

NOTES

Introduction

1. The story of Chippie is from Max Lucado, *In the Eye of the Storm* (Dallas: Word Publishing, 1991), 11.

1. Till You Do Me Right

1. Willie Dixon, "Do Me Right," *Greatest Hits*, Chess Records, c/o MCA Records, © 1955, 1983.

2. Ibid.

2. A Living Prayer

1. Adapted from James Weldon Johnson, *Creation* (New York: Holiday House, 1994).

2. C. Austin Miles, "In the Garden (I Come to the Garden Alone)," hymn no. 314, *The United Methodist Hymnal* (Nashville: The United Methodist Publishing House, 1989).

3. Mary Magdalene Could Fly!

1. See Virginia Hamilton, *The People Could Fly: American Black Folk Tales* (New York: Knopf, 1985).

2. Miles, "In the Garden."

3. Albert E. Brumley, "I'll Fly Away (When I Die, Hallelujah By and By)," Hartford Music Company, 1932.

4. Hamilton, *The People Could Fly!*

4. Not Bent or Bowed

1. Will L. Thompson, "Softly and Tenderly Jesus Is Calling," hymn no. 348, *The United Methodist Hymnal.*

2. Miles, "In the Garden."

5. An Executive Decision

1. Credit and inspiration for this chapter is due my sister, the Rev. Dr. Jessica K. Ingram.

2. Judson W. Van Deventer, "I Surrender All," hymn no. 354, *The United Methodist Hymnal.*

3. Harris Johnson, "I've Decided to Make Jesus My Choice," *Lead Me, Guide Me: The African American Catholic Hymnal* (Chicago: G.I.A. Publications, 1987).

6. Pregnant with the Promise

1. Dannibelle Hall, "Ordinary People," *The Best of Dannibelle Hall*, CGI Records, 1995.

2. Lynn Keesecker, "Yes, Lord, Yes (To Your Will and to Your Way)," Manna Music, Inc., 1983.

7. We Drink from the Well

1. Richard Blanchard, "Fill My Cup, Lord," hymn no. 641, *The United Methodist Hymnal.*

2. Johnson Oatman Jr., "No, Not One!" *Songs of Zion* (Nashville: Abingdon, 1981).

3. Charles Albert Tindley, "Beams of Heaven as I Go," hymn no. 524, *The United Methodist Hymnal.*

9. The Prodigal Daughter

1. Nina Simone, "Nobody Wants You When You Are Down and Out," *Pastel Blues: Let It All Out*, Verve Records, c/o Mercury Polygram, 1965. Emphasis added.

1998

9/06